Prai

"Once again L ... corporates to employ pe ... disabilities.

- *Addressed at business leaders here is a book that is both approachable and engaging whilst being informative and impactful.*
- *This book equips business leaders with knowledge of the topic so that they can discuss with confidence, so that they can understand the case for change and the business benefits, so they can see how to make meaningful internal and external enquiries, and so they can take practical steps from the recommendations to enable change."*

Stephen Cox, Vice President
Diversity and Inclusion Ambassador, Fujitsu

"This is a brilliant book at a time of great opportunity for every citizen of the world, and especially for people with disabilities. This book will lift up people with disabilities, and all people! Keep rockin' this world, Debra!"

John Kemp, CEO of Viscardi Center

"This is an essential read for any business leader seeking to maintain or increase market share, offering clear guidance in ensuring that the needs of all customers are considered across business processes including marketing and promotion."

David Banes, Principal at David Banes Access and Inclusion Services and former CEO, at Mada the Qatar Assistive Technology and Accessibility Center

"Debra has masterfully painted the picture of why it's not just the 'right' thing to do to hire persons with disabilities, to ensure that all online systems, both internal-facing and external-facing are accessible and inclusive to all; and, to engage in "inclusive branding" in all marketing efforts but because it's the 'smart' thing to do."

Anita Aaron, CEO
World Institute on Disability

Inclusion Branding

Revealing Secrets to Maximize ROI

By Debra Ruh

Ruh Global, LLC
18122 Vontay Road
Rockville, Virginia 23146
debra@ruhglobal.com

Printed in the United States
ISBN: 978-1-7320432-0-6 (paperback)
978-1-7320432-1-3 (ebook)

Note from the Author:

Because of the dynamic nature of the internet, any web addresses or links included in this book may have changed since publication and may no longer be valid.

The views and opinions expressed in this book are solely my own and do not reflect the views or opinions of my employers or the organization.

Dedication

This book is dedicated to my mother, Sara Frances Newsom. She left this world on Dec 31, 2017. My mother inspired me to become a writer and to champion people that are disenfranchised. She is loved and missed.

Table of Contents

Foreword.. ix

Introduction xvii

1 - Inclusive Marketing and Branding................ 1

2 - Communities.. 25

3 - Creating Engagement 45

4 - Risks... 67

5 - Understand the Community and Building
Brand Ambassadors.................................... 79

6 - Best Practices 97

About Debra Ruh 127

Foreword

by Patrick Romzek,

IT Expert and Father of son with Down syndrome

This book is not about social justice, but rather a business imperative that is impacting our world as we speak. This profound book has the ability to transform the contributions people with disabilities can make in our communities, homes, and across our global workplaces.

People with disabilities should be a cornerstone of every business strategy. Why? First, while every company seeks new, expanded, and incremental markets and market segments to drive product and business growth, people with disabilities represent a huge and largely untapped business growth opportunity. Second, as unemployment rates decline and businesses seek new sources of talent, people with disabilities represent a massive untapped pool of productive and reliable talent, that, contrary to popular belief, can perform many jobs as well as, or better than other candidates.

Most importantly, as businesses focus on fiercely protecting and growing their global brand equity, disability inclusion represents a huge brand opportunity to drive global business, and brand growth—or organizations risk not being labeled as disability friendly.

Disability inclusion is an opportunity for every company to do both well and good for their business, employees, shareholders, and society. People with disabilities are a significant force in society, historically underappreciated, but thanks to new technology, they are an emerging global economic force. Like innovators finding an unmet need, companies and countries WILL discover the business potential of people with disabilities. Many already have.

To begin the journey, every business leader should read **Inclusion Branding** by Debra Ruh to understand the breadth, depth, and global opportunities disability inclusion represents for their **business and their brand**. Many companies include disability inclusion initiatives as part of their diversity and corporate social responsibility strategies. I advocate another point of view, one that recognizes that disability inclusion can be a critical business imperative that drives future business growth and sustainability.

No viable and sustainable business strategy from a market-leading company could succeed without being inclusive of all population groups. A business would not exist if it intentionally excluded critical populations from its workforce or business strategy. People with disabilities are the largest minority group in

America, according to Disability Funders Network. However, this community is not as well organized, appreciated, or represented as other minority populations today. With Debra Ruh illuminating the potential of workforce strategies on people with disabilities, and major global brands like Tommy Hilfiger and Microsoft mining this opportunity, it is only a matter of time before large and small companies alike follow these visionary leaders through their brands and products.

Debra Ruh is an accomplished, highly respected, and influential leader in the disability community. She deeply understands the potential for people with disabilities. Her personal experiences as a special needs parent have imbued her with deep wisdom, and an understanding of why people with disabilities embrace certain products and brands. She personally realizes the potential people with disabilities represent, from a business point of view.

As a leading advisor to major global organizations (businesses and governments), Debra has demonstrated her commitment to helping organizations realize the economic and brand potentials businesses can derive from disability inclusion. With her guidance, global brands have a steadfast activist who stands ready to advocate for their business and brand benefits.

In this book, Debra generously shares her insights and expertise on how, with disability inclusion, businesses can realize significant opportunities for themselves, society and communities. Her real-world examples provide insight and underscore the vast employee and marketplace potential people with disabilities represent. I can attest to this opportunity from my own experiences, both personal and professional.

I am also a parent of a special needs child, who has blessed me with a deep respect and understanding of the potential for people with disabilities. As a special needs parent, I understand and share the deep emotional loyalty for brands, organizations, and products that make the lives of people with disabilities better.

My son, Andrew, was born with Down syndrome and was gravely ill throughout his first year of life. He has overcome life-saving surgery and survived near-death experiences. These deeply personal and challenging experiences caused me to build advocacy for and visceral loyalty to organizations and products that helped him, our family, and other people with disabilities. For my son, these experiences helped him forge a deep well of strengths and characteristics I did not see in others who had not weathered these challenges.

Andrew is developmentally challenged and cannot read or write, but he has an unrelenting perseverance, an unquenchable spirit, and an extraordinarily positive attitude and thirst for life. It occurred to me that these characteristics are also evident in high-performing employees. This experience led me to better understand and explore the potential for people with disabilities in the workforce. What I discovered, however, was shocking and disturbing. And it inspired me to make a difference.

As a senior leader in the IT industry for over 30 years, I have witnessed first-hand the many challenges companies face on a daily basis. For instance, I have faced the challenge of finding new sources of talent in an ever-shrinking global talent pool that is increasingly complex to hire, train and retain. I have also experienced the challenges of building brand equity, then watching how quickly it can be lost.

One of my earliest roles was working for a vertical industry market leader with a solid customer loyalty base and growing brand equity. Despite these advantages, the company lost brand value and equity in a relatively short period of time through a series of strategic missteps, because they simply did not understand that perception in the marketplace is everything.

As I began to assess the potential for disability inclusion in the workforce, I came to realize the tragic state of lifelong unemployment for people with disabilities. Globally, one billion people have a disability, and approximately 80 percent are unemployed. Only 36 percent of people with disabilities in the U.S. have a job, and only one in five have a full-time job. Sadly, one out of every three people with disabilities lives in poverty. Surprisingly, 50 percent of people with disabilities with an advanced degree are also unemployed, according to the U.S. Department of Labor (2016).

Armed with this knowledge, I clearly understood the challenges people with disabilities face in the workforce, and I made a commitment to make a difference. I became involved as a volunteer and board member in a number of disability-focused organizations and used my business and personal experiences to drive disability inclusion innovation and to accelerate disability employment.

Through my journey advocating for people with disabilities, and driving innovation in disability inclusion and employment, I had the pleasure to meet and work with Debra Ruh and recognize the great work she is doing. What I have learned through my experiences mirrors many of the examples, premises, and insights shared by Debra in this book.

1. People with disabilities are indeed a large pool of untapped talent for businesses seeking exceptional talent. As many companies struggle to find new sources of talent in a shrinking labor pool with historically low unemployment, there is a vast pool of exceptional talent that is able, ready and willing to deliver extraordinary results, starting today. Some people with disabilities require accommodations; but this is insignificant in comparison to the value these employees add to our workforce, business, culture, communities, and lives.

2. Disability inclusion is good for a company's brand. Debra illustrates this point extensively in this book. The brand potential for disability products and services is enormous because people with disabilities and their families are keenly aware of how these brands strive to make their lives better. In exchange, these companies benefit from strong brand loyalty and lifelong customers.

3. Having a company-wide product and brand focus on people with disabilities is good for society, and equally as im-

portant, it's really good for business. People with disabilities who are employed represent an untapped market: like traditional consumers, they can buy our products, drive customer success, and engage our employees.

4. Making disability inclusion a visible priority and driving awareness of it creates an emotional connection with employees and like-minded customers. Employees want to work for a company that is doing both well financially and good in the world. Customers want to buy from companies that share their values.

5. Disability inclusion changes lives. Being employed at something we are good at can contribute to, make a difference in, and build self-esteem, economic self-sufficiency, self-worth and financial security. This is something we all strive for, and it's something people with disabilities seek, too. This is why employment for people with disabilities is transformational–it not only changes the employee, it also changes their co-workers, their customers, and communities, and all the other lives they touch.

In summary, disability inclusion is an opportunity to "change the world." What is less obvious is that disability inclusion is an amazing and emerging opportunity for business—to increase brand equity, drive business growth, and create an untapped new source of customers and employees. Debra's groundbreaking insights and practical advice in this book have more business potential than many of the strategies employed by businesses today.

In the words of Thomas Edison, "The reason a lot of people do not recognize opportunity is because it usually goes around wearing overalls looking like hard work." People with disabilities are your neighbor in overalls that you may not think about. With Debra's insights, the right focus, and a bit of hard work, we can each take the first steps towards understanding the great potential people with disabilities represent to our business, our workforce, and our brand. Working together, we can change the way the world embraces and appreciates people with disabilities.

Introduction

by Richard Schatzberg

Chairman, Ruh Global Communications

Chief Commercial Officer, NeST Technologies

I have been involved in the disabilities community for over twenty years. And the one thing that I believe most is that each wave of technology and societal innovation offers the community of people with disabilities an opportunity for, not just inclusion, but leadership. In the past, these opportunities have passed us by, leaving us to play "catch-up" or act retroactively to the changes that these innovations create. As an example, Section 508 of the Rehabilitation Act of 1974, as amended in 1998, is a reactive measure that was used to ensure that people with disabilities were not left out of the electronics and information technology (E&IT) revolution. But all these years later, many government websites and systems still do not meet this standard.

Today, we face an enormous wave of innovation, across many areas that is bound to change the way we live, work, play and communicate. Everything from artificial intelligence, social media, the digital economy and currencies, wearable internet of things (IoT) devices, and the "gig" economy will impact our lives in unprecedented ways.

I've played various leadership roles in businesses, mostly technology businesses, for more years than I care to admit. The intersection of my personal and business lives forged my belief that these waves of technology innovation can significantly and positively impact people with disabilities from a community, an education, and a workplace standpoint. However, there remains much about the disabilities community that has stayed the same for quite some time, and that is unfortunate.

For example, the employment rates of people with disabilities have not increased fast enough, even with the passage of the Americans with Disabilities Act in 1990, and the fact that people with disabilities have incredibly employable attributes. Further, the fragmentation of the marketplace is something our community has dealt with perpetually. Our community has five basic community sectors: (1) blind and low vision; (2) deaf and hard of hearing; (3) intellectual or cognitive; (4) physical or mobility; and (5) mental health. You could even say we have six sectors if you include the aging population.

Within each of these community segments, there is additional sub-fragmentation. For example, within the intellectual or cognitive sector, we have the autistic spectrum. And within the autistic spectrum, we have a wide array of autistic severity. Within these sub-fragments, there is a long history of non-profits, such as the American Asperger's Association, that are specific to various segments of this global community. Although the work that is done by these non-profits is absolutely amazing, the incredible fragmentation that exists within the community has, in my mind, been something that has in many cases held back the community.

When we consider the global population of people with disabilities, including the aging population, as well as family members and caregivers, we're talking about anywhere between one out of every five, maybe one out of every six people on the planet. In total, the consolidated population represents more than one billion people. That's a massive global population. The power of our community lies in our scale, and in the incredibly powerful attributes of its members. Yet, there has always been the breakdown of that community through this fragmentation and sub-fragmentation.

When I joined forces with Debra Ruh as the Chairman of Ruh Global Communications, we hoped that these problems could be solved through innovation, solid communications strategies, and advances in technology. For example, social media is critical to breaking the barriers down and creating a community that is reachable. Too often this community is viewed from a charitable or corporate social responsibility (CSR) standpoint. Charitable activity is at the core of my family's activities. We very much believe in the power of giving and of servant leadership. However, all of the great charity work that has been done, and will continue to be done, has not advanced or empowered the community in scale.

What we really need is for businesses to view people with disabilities as a population, a market segment, that is reachable, and that has incredibly powerful attributes. What's amazing about the global community of people with disabilities, this 1.2 billion strong population, is that it covers all age spectrums, all ethnicities, all geographic areas, genders, religious preferences, etc. Disabilities do not discriminate.

A few years ago, Debra Ruh and I reconnected. I was involved in a foundation called Runway of Dreams, founded by Mindy Scheier, who lives in my hometown of Livingston, New Jersey. I read about Mindy on Facebook, and about what she was trying to accomplish in the fashion industry. After meeting Mindy, my wife and I decided to get involved. Mindy's goal was to create an adaptive clothing line for kids with disabilities. Kids with disabilities, especially physical disabilities, often have challenges with traditional clothing.

Eventually, Runway of Dreams connected with an amazing brand, Tommy Hilfiger. Gary Sheinbaum and his team at Tommy were very excited about getting involved, but with some hesitancy. Although they loved the concept, they were unsure of how to properly reach and communicate with the community. Imagine the courage and vision of Gary and his team in leaping forward on a project like this. After all, no other brand, to my knowledge, had ever attempted this. John Kemp, CEO of the Viscardi Center, and I quickly reassured the Tommy team that we would take the lead in spreading the word about this adaptive clothing line in an inclusive and appropriate manner. We reached out to Debra Ruh, Joyce Bender and several other great friends in this amazing community, and asked for help in promoting this line of adaptive clothing.

The adaptive clothing line launched on February 22, 2016, as a pilot project and within about a week, the line was selling quickly via Tommy.com. I had always known that Debra Ruh was a social media leader. But until this activity, I didn't understand the scale of her reach. Although so many people contributed to the success of the trial, I give an enormous amount of credit to Debra Ruh and her amazing team at Ruh Global Communications. As I started to receive the analytics on her team's activities in support of the Tommy Adaptive Clothing line, I began to recognize that social media provided the opportunity to break down the artificial barriers that had been in place for so long. Social media could connect this community into a cohesive, powerful force. Soon after, I joined Ruh Global as Chairman to help see this outcome to fruition.

Our community needs to be treated as consumers. Not to sound too much like Gordon Gekko in the movie Wall Street, but profit is the driver of corporations. Profit, or the prospect thereof, determines levels of investments, strategies and success or failure. At Ruh Global, our mission is to help corporations view the community of people with disabilities as product/service consumers and as prospective employees. We hope corporations will stop viewing their work within this community as charity or as part of a corporate social responsibility program. While well intentioned and powerful, history has shown that it just isn't enough. We need something bigger.

On occasion, I have heard consumers with disabilities say that corporations should not seek to make a profit from the community. I could not disagree with this sentiment more. It is only through the view of people with disabilities as a viable, vibrant, and strong community that outcomes will begin to change. Like any other consumer, we have the right to purchase products from companies and brands that we admire. If a product is outside of our price reach, just like every other consumer, we have the right not to buy that product.

The same is true on the employment side. When it comes to employing people with disabilities, we want people to achieve their work status and personal goals based upon their capabilities, not as a result of an act of charity. We want employers to hire people with disabilities because they have great skills and capabilities. End of the story!

People with disabilities have been great contributors to a culture and community because they have incredibly great sense of humor and positive attitudes. Does that mean everyone in the community has those attributes? Of course not. But as a general characteristic within the community, people with disabilities are great problem solvers and have great empathy for others. These are the kinds of employees I want in my company, and many corporations are starting to recognize that. People with disabilities tend to think outside of the box and to find solutions to issues and problems that other people have not found. If we can find a way as a civilization to tap into that, we'll be better off.

Debra Ruh's message is important to our community of persons with disabilities as well as for business brands. We need to ensure that this wave of innovation does not pass by without us taking a proactive leadership position. The time for our community to engage is measured in days, weeks and months, not years. It is now that we must call upon the power and scale of our community, and our leaders, to ensure that we are an active player in how these technologies can create inclusion and opportunity for our community. More than ever before, we can leverage our strengths that can be seen as a differentiation and take on roles that have been closed off to us for generations. We can use this opportunity to create wealth within our community and to overcome the ever-present correlation between disability and poverty.

Disability is the new cool. Now is the time for our community to accept with vigor a new position in society. And Debra Ruh and her team at Ruh Global are leading that charge.

1

Inclusive Marketing and Branding

"Inclusion Branding: The energy you expend on tearing down any negative perceptions others may have of you in the area of inclusion could have been much better spent building your brand as an inclusive leader, employer or organization. Plus, it is more fun and rewarding building your positive brand versus defending one that is not so positive."

-Kevin Bradley, The Boeing Company, Senior Manager, Global Workforce Inclusion

Introduction

Let's define Inclusive Marketing and Branding for the purpose of this book. In this book, I am defining inclusive marketing to include any underserved population like persons with disabilities, indigenous people, and LGBTQ+ communities. Mainstream advertisers have not always included these segments in their marketing and branding efforts. Slowly that has started to change and evolve, but we have a lot of work to do.

Over a billion people around the world have disabilities. That means over a billion people around the world, and their families, are making consumer-purchasing decisions every day, looking for products that meet their unique and specific needs, as well as products that are not related to ability. When these consumers' product needs go unmet because brands aren't reaching them with strategic marketing campaigns or aren't creating the products in the first place, countless dollars are being left on the table: And when these consumers buy everyday products from indiscriminate brands because they can find no inclusive brand to give their loyalty to, that translates to more missed profits for you.

My husband, daughter and myself are proud to be part of the community of persons with disabilities. That gives me the insight to work globally to help corporate brands understand how to effectively include individuals with disabilities in your workforce, customer base, and other stakeholder positions. In this chapter, we will explore why Social Impact matters for your bottom line and how it ties into inclusion of persons with disabilities or other underserved groups.

Next, we will explore Impact Branding, the 4 P's (Profit, People, Purpose, and Planet), United Nations Sustainable Development Goals (SDGs), and finally Disruption to show how these factors are changing the way societies are looking at the issues and how many expect corporate brands to respond. It might be confusing mixing Social Impact with Disruption, but we will discuss how these factors are changing the world in many positive and hopeful ways.

It is an exciting and sometimes scary time in our world. I believe that humanity is trying to evolve and brands are a huge part of these efforts. In the past, we have turned to government to solve societal problems like disability inclusion. However, I believe corporate brands are going to affect greater change in society.

Why Social Impact Matters

There are almost eight billion people living in our world. According to World Health Organization, one in seven people around the world has a disability. That means persons with disabilities represent over a billion people. The world is changing, and many people feel it is time for a call to action. Brands that want to be taken seriously need to understand that customers (often called consumers) want to do business with companies that are adding value to their families and lives, as opposed to ignoring or leaving their needs to be fulfilled by others.

There are many complex problems in our world today: disenfranchised people, disease, animal cruelty, climate change, hunger, violence, terrorism, lack of education, digital divide, and employment inequities to name a few. Societies expect corporations to have positive social impact on these situations.

All generations expect positive impacts, but the younger generations have vowed to only support brands that are making a positive difference in the world. They have clearly stated in various studies that they are willing to pay more money to do business with brands that have a positive social impact.

There are also growing expectations that brands have diverse workforces that include persons with disabilities. The workforce is changing, and so are employee values, thus, keeping employees satisfied has never been more important. Workers expect their employers to align business goals with positive social impact as part of their Corporate Social Responsibility (CSR), which should align with an impact agenda dedicated to the mission of the brand. The Nielsen June 2014 report "Doing Well by Doing Good"[1] showed that 67% of millennials want to work for a socially responsible brand.

Some companies have been in-tune with this trend, such as Deloitte (which has been doing a report on millennials for several years). The Deloitte 2015 Millennial Report showed 75% of millennials believe their employers should be more focused on social impact that will help improve society.[2] Interestingly, in its 2017 report, Deloitte numbers show that millennials are not as confident; many are apprehensive and seeking stability and opportunities in an uncertain world.

---

1 http://www.nielsen.com/content/dam/nielsenglobal/jp/docs/report/2014/Nielsen Global Corporate Social Responsibility Report - June 2014.pdf

2 https://www2.deloitte.com/content/dam/Deloitte/global/Documents/About-Deloitte/gx-wef-2015-millennial-survey-executivesummary.pdf

"This group is increasingly taking on senior positions that provide platforms for promoting working environments and practices seen as most likely to address society's challenges. The Millennial Survey sets out the concerns of millennials, their expectations for the future, and how they believe business might help create the type of world they wish to inhabit. The outside world might be increasingly unstable, but millennials give reason to believe that, by working together, there is hope to improve performance of both business, as well as society as a whole."[3]

Societal expectations for businesses to support the communities where they do business are on the rise and inclusion of disenfranchised members of the societies is part of those expectations. We have seen those expectations in our religious and spiritual communities as illustrated in the Dali Lama's observation, "Technology that is available to us today should be utilized across the globe. But ultimately the solution lies within compassion. If we have compassion for the planet and compassion for everybody that inhabits it, we will do the right thing." Now we are seeing those expectations reach the marketplace, which opens up new opportunities for you to appeal to and attract an expanded customer base.

[3] https://www2.deloitte.com/global/en/pages/about-deloitte/articles/deloitte-millennial-survey-research-scope.html

Two Inclusion Strategies for Social Impact: #1 Hiring Inclusively

Including persons with disabilities as employees is the first and most obvious way to demonstrate that your brand is making a positive difference in the world in regards to inclusivity and to connect with the compassion of consumers. Persons with disabilities all over the world want to be independent, have families, become taxpayers, and contribute to society. You can be the brand that provides avenues for fulfilling these dreams, and the great news is that this community is an untapped resource that is eager and able to work.

Consumer attitudes toward companies that hire individuals with disabilities were assessed through a national public survey in the U.S. In a poll funded by the Department of Education NIDRR[4], 92 percent of consumers felt more favorable toward those that hire individuals with disabilities. The participants also had strong positive beliefs about the value and benefits of hiring people with disabilities, with 87 percent "specifically agreeing that they would prefer to give their business to companies that hire individuals with disabilities."[5]

Another benefit to hiring inclusively is that employees with disabilities bring unique experiences that can help transform a workplace and enhance products and services. This is because persons with disabilities must overcome many physical and digi-

---

[4] http://www.worksupport.com/documents/romano_siperstein.pdf

[5] Journal of Vocational Rehabilitation, 24(1), 3-9, Siperstein, G. N., Romano, N., Mohler, A., & Parker, R. (2006).

tal accessibility barriers, such as websites or intranet that are not designed to be accessible, or images that are not tagged for screen readers. Because of these challenges, employees with disabilities often create elaborate systems and tools to help simplify their lives in creative ways. They develop a different and often stronger relationship with their employer than the average employee and come with unique technical strengths.

According to a study done by DePaul University, employees with disabilities are hard workers, innovative, dependable, and loyal to their employers.

> *"Participants noted low absenteeism rates and long tenures," the study explained. "They also described their employees with disabilities as loyal, reliable, and hardworking. An additional benefit to hiring people with disabilities was the diversification of work settings, which led to an overall positive work environment." DePaul University*[6]

Employers benefit by hiring people for their unique talents and potential contributions, regardless of disability. That makes hiring a person with a disability a bonus in today's knowledge economy, where diverse skills, opinions, and insights offer a competitive edge, especially when persons with disabilities make up such a large part of the consumer population that brands are competing for in today's market.

---

[6] http://www.forbes.com/sites/judyowen/2012/05/12/a-cost-benefit-analysis-of-disability-in-the-workplace/

Remember, the world is a diverse place, and the more we include those who are different from us, the more society wins. What if a baby born with severe disabilities were the one to finally cure cancer or create the technology that allows society to unlock some wonder of the world? Today's consumer believes in this possibility and knows that the assumption that persons with disabilities do not have dreams, hopes, and desires, including wanting to have significant accomplishments in their lives, is simply underestimating them. In fact, some find it insulting to assume a person's disabilities define their ability to meet their life goals and have impact.

Disabilities are a natural part of the human condition, and the emerging socially conscious consumer doesn't want to define a person by one dimension of their humanness. This consumer already believes that having a visible or invisible disability does not mean a person is broken, unwilling, or unable to contribute, and you can show them that your brand is keeping up with, or even leading this evolution of consciousness, by hiring inclusively. Bottom line: Employing persons with disabilities not only expands your pool of possible talent, it is smart business.

Two Inclusion Strategies for Social Impact: #2 Marketing Inclusively

The second way to include persons with disabilities is less obvious in terms of demonstrating your social impact, though no less significant in the actual impact that you make, but more obvious in terms of boosting your profit margin, so it's a win/win. By including persons with disabilities as part of your target customer base, you make a meaningful difference by showing this underserved population that they are wanted, valued and significant. Many of your other customers will recognize this contribution for themselves, but some will need to have it pointed out, which we will discuss in the remaining sections of this chapter. And in terms of profit, it goes without saying that having new customers is desirable.

My family, like many in the world, has been impacted (often in positive ways) by disabilities. One significant impact is the way having family members with disabilities has influenced how we spend our consumer dollars. I have an adult daughter named Sara who was born with Trisomy 21 (also known as Down syndrome), and both my parents became disabled later in life. As a consumer, I notice which companies make their entrances accessible, their websites accessible, whether they use individuals with disabilities in their marketing campaigns, and other efforts they make to include or not include my family members with disabilities. I remember shopping in Kohl's one holiday season, and they had a mannequin in a wheelchair. It made me proud to shop at Kohl's.

I chose to change pharmacies after a 20-year relationship with a retail pharmacy company in the United States because they did little to nothing to include persons with disabilities in their marketing and employment efforts. Plus, their website was terribly inaccessible to many of my friends who are blind or cannot use their hands. I was pleased with every other aspect of my shopping experience there, but I knew of Walgreens'[7] efforts to include people with intellectual disabilities in their distribution centers, and I made the switch.

Their success at including these individuals has benefited not only their employees with disabilities but also their company, by expanding their pool of possible hires as well as their market. They are making other efforts to ensure accessibility of their products as well, such as adding large-print prescriptions and talking prescription bottles. As a result, I changed my buying behavior to reward their efforts. The studies cited above suggest that many other customers would do the same, given adequate information and opportunity.

In addition, my husband of 35 years recently got hearing aids after learning he has a significant hearing loss. He hesitated for years before getting hearing aids because of stigmas in his own mind. After wearing the hearing aids for a few days, he told me that it changed his world for the better and wondered what took him so long to make the decision. My husband is just one example of a missed marketing opportunity in which marketing could have brought awareness to the benefits of a hearing aid years earlier, and impact branding could have eliminated the stigma.

He joins the other 72 million baby boomers learning that as we age, many of us acquire disabilities. Your brand has the opportunity to inspire us to believe that this does not mean we are

[7] http://www.walgreens.com

broken and to demonstrate how assistive technology can improve our daily lives. Showing us that assistive technologies allow generations to 'Age in Place' more comfortably and with dignity has social impact and fiscal rewards. We will spend our money on that, for ourselves and our loved ones.

Further, you can be the brand that tells the world that having a disability — whether born with it or acquired — does not mean you are broken and of no value to society. You can convey the message that as human beings, disabilities are a normal part of life. As that brand, you make a social impact and attract not just persons with disabilities and their families as loyal customers, but also the emerging socially conscious consumer.

What is Impact Branding?

Social media can hijack a brand by exponentially sharing a story (also called trending), but trending on social media is not always a positive experience. Once this type of situation occurs, the propagated story sometimes has little to do with the actual event.

We are in a time of sensationalized slash-and-burn social media. It seemingly does not matter if the stories are true as long as the end result is everyone is upset on social media and the story trends. In these situations, the brand image can be damaged, and the company has to execute damage control and reactive measures.

Here are a few examples of brands having social media blunders.

Seoul Secret created a marketing campaign[8] for their skin-lightening cosmetics called: "White makes you win." The brand created a tweet referring to the campaign along with a video of actress and singer Chris Horwang talking about her career and how her white skin helped her to be so successful. As you can imagine, the ad created a massive backlash.

Another example of an offensive tweet[9] was created by MTV Australia. They tweeted comments about the clarity of the English spoken by America Ferrera and Eva Longoria while they were on stage at the Golden Globes. If you are not familiar with these talented actresses, they are both from Mexico and have Spanish accents. MTV Australia issued an apology, but that did not appease the angry tweets. They released another apology, but the angry tweets continued. Now we use it as a lesson learned. Some tweets never go away.

Another example is an advertisement used in a political campaign in the United States; the GOP sent out a tweet[10] accusing Senator Tammy Duckworth, a Democrat from the State of Illinois, of not 'standing up' for veterans. Although this is typical of political mudslinging in American political campaigns, it crossed

---

[8] https://www.theguardian.com/world/video/2016/jan/08/whiteness-is-winning-thai-ad-promotes-skin-whitening-pills-video
[9] https://www.theguardian.com/film/2016/jan/11/mtv-australia-under-fire-for-racist-tweet-during-golden-globe-awards
[10] https://www.cnn.com/2016/03/08/politics/tammy-duckworth-nrsc-tweet-deleted-veterans/index.html

a line because Senator Duckworth had served as a United States Army Lieutenant Colonel and lost both her legs while serving in Iraq. She even came back and worked as Assistant Secretary in the Department of Veterans Affairs. They also posted the tweet on International Women's Day. There was a major backlash on social media from many communities and individuals. The community of persons with disabilities, service members and veterans and other Americans were very upset and took to social media to express their anger over the insensitive remarks.

In the early days of social media and blogging, Nestle was being criticized for endangering animal habitats, and it reacted by sending a cease-and-desist order to bloggers and social media influencers. In the past, this type of activity was part of many brands' efforts to stop the public from saying negative things about their brand. However, the rules have changed in the age of social media. The cease-and-desist order backfired when the bloggers retaliated with their social media mechanisms, thus causing the company brand more damage. [11]

It is hard being under the microscope all the time, and we all make mistakes. Social media is unforgiving when brands make a mistake, and the best thing you can do in this situation is to apologize quickly and sincerely.

Your brand can take proactive action to maintain a positive image and avoid mistakes by putting more facts behind your thinking and decision-making. One way to do this is via brand

---

[11] http://dg3tb7gs.myq-see.com/nestle-infant-formula-case-study-answers1037-f2.html

impact market research, which is a method used to establish the effectiveness of advertising and messaging for a particular brand, product, or service. And it's important to note that in the present day, brand messages and marketing is increasingly linked with the digital world, especially social media.[12]

You may find that like many brands you care about impact branding, also known as a social impact strategy, and aim to blend these efforts into your corporate social responsibility (CSR) policies. These mechanisms should be designed in a way that can help improve the overall mission and complement your unique identity. Like other business strategies, it should include:

- Corporate objectives
- Definitive social impact goals
- Quantifiable business outcomes
- Measurable public deliverables to assure success
- Marketing and communications strategies

These must be developed with connotations of positive bottom-line impact and revenue generation because if it's considered a charity model, it will eventually become non-viable due to funding issues.

[12] www.djsresearch.co.uk/glossary/item/Brand-Impact-Market-Research

Inclusive Marketing and Branding

The 4 P's for Focus

Corporations must be profitable to survive, but society has additional expectations. Businesses need to support their employees and customers, have sustainable business practices, and engage their communities by having positive social impact on their local, national, and global communities. These focuses can be represented by the titles **People, Planet, Profit, and Purpose.**

In today's world, your brand needs to show the public that you stand for something besides profit. Many brands are making a difference in their communities, but they do not share the stories. Many people assume that corporations only focus on areas where they make the most money. It is very important for your brand to tell your social responsibility stories and to focus on social impact in your entire footprint. These stories are not just for your annual reports. If the community does not know about your efforts – your impact will not be as powerful as it could be for your brand and the communities you care about.

Let's look at an example. Multi-National brands that want persons with disabilities in your workforce can join the United Nations' International Labor Organization (ILO)[13]. The ILO is deeply committed to full inclusion of all people in the workforce. They created the Global Business and Disability Network to support B2B conversations and help multi-national corporations understand that a diverse workforce includes persons with disabili-

[13] http://www.ilo.org/

ties and focuses on the Four P Principles of Social Impact: People, Planet, Purpose, and Profit.

Sustainable Development Goals (SDGs)

Even national brands have global vendors and partners, so all brands should consider being part of the United Nations (UN) Sustainable Development Goals (SDGs) that are designed to support the world. "The Sustainable Development Goals" (SDGs), officially known as Transforming our World: the 2030 Agenda for Sustainable Development, is a set of seventeen "Global Goals" with 169 targets between them."[14]

It is important to note that the SDGs are part of the United Nations Development Group,[15] an independent campaign known as Project Everyone.[16] The group introduced the term Global Goals, and this campaign was supported by corporate institutions and other international organizations. When companies join this critical global movement, we can all collectively accelerate the agenda to make the planet healthier and make the world a more inclusive place for everyone.

---

14 https://en.wikipedia.org/wiki/Sustainable_Development_Goals

15 https://en.wikipedia.org/wiki/United_Nations_Development_Group

16 http://www.project-everyone.org/

Disruption

The world is experiencing disruption at so many levels that sometimes it is exhausting. The industry of disability inclusion and accessibility is also in the middle of disruption. Disruption can be painful, but it is necessary to have disruption in order to grow to the next level. The key to disruptive innovation that works is customers. Your goal is to help customers fall in love with your brand.

You can foster this affection with inclusion and accessibility service innovations. These best practices help your team assure that all customers including persons with disabilities have the access they need. It begins at the pre-design stage and follows the entire design life cycle, with every process created, incorporating accessibility and disability inclusion into your policies, services, and products. These efforts support all customers, even the most demanding customers. It also allows team members to proactively innovate and solve problems before they surface.

That's where the innovation lives. That's how disruptive innovation works, by surprising and delighting people when least expected. We know that we're already designing smart cities, driverless cars, internet of things, robots. Disney is a good example of embracing a whole experience. They don't have employees; they have cast members. They don't have customers; they have guests, and all guests should get to experience the magic. Everyone. Your brand can create disruption like this in your own unique way.

Interview with Malcom Glenn[17]

An example of a brand that has created disruption is Uber. We discussed many of these topics during an interview with Malcom Glenn, Strategic Partnerships with Uber, about disruption and inclusion. Uber has also had major brand challenges including some that caused Travis Kalanick, Uber's CEO to step down in June 2017. Here are some highlights from my interview and additional information from my research on Uber.

It is hard to believe that Uber has only been around since 2009. The young company has accomplished many things, created disruption in the transportation industry but along the way made some huge mistakes. It was interesting to review the internal investigation report[18] led by Former Attorney General, Eric Holder's group. I commend many of the suggestions including changing Chief Diversity Officer position to Chief Diversity and Inclusion Officer. The expanded role has the potential to allow Uber to expand their efforts with inclusion. The report recommended the position report directly to the CEO or the COO. I agree with that recommendation because corporate brands have not taken these roles seriously. The Chief Diversity Officer, Chief Accessibility Officer, Diversity and Inclusion Officers positions are usually middle management, with no budget or resources.

---

17 http://www.ruhglobal.com/63-uber-supporting-diversity-inclusion/

18 http://fortune.com/2017/06/13/uber-internal-investigation-results-public/

Often these roles have great desire to create change for the company but rarely have the resources or authority to create real change.

It is important to note that Uber has three constituencies. (1) The constituencies that make up their employee population. (2) The riders that use their product every day. (3) The drivers without whom they would not be able to have a product. Uber's current Global Head of Diversity and Inclusion, is named Bernard Coleman. His team focuses on global diversity in the biggest sense of the word, diversity by LGBTQ status, diversity for people with disabilities, people of color, women, and geographic diversity. Uber is working on instituting blind resume reviews, whereby you don't see the name of the person at the top, so you can't necessarily have unconscious biases creeping in as you evaluate candidates.

They have also made a commitment to focus on diversity and inclusive of their drivers. For example, one of the things that they instituted a few years ago is a series of app features that make it easier for people who are deaf or hard-of-hearing to drive for the Uber platform. For point of reference, current Uber drivers have a traditional app setting that provides an audible ping when you get matched with a rider.

Uber understood that the ping would not work for people who are deaf or hard-of-hearing, so they changed the app to allow the rider to see a flash on the screen instead of an audible ping. When they're matched with that rider, the rider gets a notification that says: 'Your driver may be deaf or hard-of-hearing and the phone function is disabled'. So instead of the rider trying to call their driver, they text that driver. The passenger is required to input their GPS, so the driver doesn't have to try to listen to instructions. These small updates allow the platform to be more inclusive for drivers with different abilities and disabilities.

Uber has made efforts to increase accessibility for riders who may have disabilities. The Uber app is completely accessible for voiceover and talk back on iOS and Android. Plus, they instituted a number of communications to drivers around the requirements to accept service animals. Every single driver in the United States, get an in-app notification reminding them of their requirements both under the Uber policy and under the American's with Disabilities Act (ADA) to accept all service animals.

Uber has a lot of work to do to assure wheelchair-accessible vehicles. The challenge is that due to the nature of the Uber model, where drivers use their own cars on their own time they do need to solve these issues. They have a program in about 12 different U.S. cities that have some form of wheelchair-accessible vehicle program and partnerships with taxis to allow riders to request a wheelchair-accessible taxi. They also partner with commercial providers allowing them to use vehicles that accept wheelchairs on the Uber platform. It is also interesting to note that in a handful of cities they are hoping to institute and scale a leasing model. So if someone is looking to drive with Uber and they do not have a car, they can actually get a car through a leasing organization, and instead of giving those folks a standard Toyota Prius or a Honda Civic, they've made the leasing terms for wheelchair-accessible vehicles a little bit better to encourage more wheelchair-accessible vehicles.

Innovative and disruptive models like Uber can add great value to people wanting to 'Age in Place'. My late 91-year-old father-in-law had his driver's license revoked by the state of Florida. Our family had to file a complaint saying that we thought he was a danger to himself and others on the road. This was after he had driven himself to his doctor's appointment at 1:00 in the morning instead of the afternoon. His driving skills had deteriorated, and it had gotten to the point where it was dangerous for him to be driving. Our family had to take action, but it broke his heart losing his license and, in his eyes, his independence.

My 30-year-old daughter, Sara Ruh, born with Down syndrome, has never learned to drive because of her intellectual disabilities. It appears that programs like Uber and Lyft can allow her more independence at least in regards to transportation.

Uber and Lyft are beginning to change the culture of how people think about moving around. Individual car ownership is such an integral part of the American lifestyle and story. Self-driving cars are a focal point of Uber's attention. Uber has pilots in two cities, Tempe, Arizona, and Pittsburgh, Pennsylvania, using autonomous or self-driving cars on the road today.

Uber's vision is to have a fleet model, and so some people are doing development into self-driving cars, but they believe that people will still purchase their own cars, and that might happen to some degree, but it's probably not all or nothing. But we believe that the most efficient and affordable way that people will adopt self-driving cars is on top of the existing ride-hailing model that we have today. You can imagine some of the benefits of that, right? The most significant is how many lives will be saved.

Over 1 million people die every single year in traffic accidents, and 94% of traffic accidents are the result of human error[19]. What if you could, obviously, completely eliminate that? That would be absolutely miraculous. But what if you could even just significantly decrease the number of people who die every year in car accidents? That would have a massive positive impact on society.

According to an article[20] by David Morris, reports of the death of car buying among millennials turn out to have been greatly exaggerated. But there's one big reason ride-hailing services like Uber, and eventually, autonomous vehicles, are still a threat to private car ownership. Put simply, we just don't use our cars very much. Transportation adviser Paul Barter has confirmed longstanding claims by urban planners that, on average, cars are parked 95% of the time[21]. Barter tries three different approaches, first using data on the number of car trips and their average time, then survey results about the time we spend driving, and finally extrapolates from reports on the distance and speeds

---

19 http://cyberlaw.stanford.edu/blog/2013/12/human-error-cause-vehicle-crashes

20 http://www.bloombergview.com/articles/2016-01-04/millennials-are-buying-cars-after-all

21 http://www.reinventingparking.org/2013/02/cars-are-parked-95-of-time-lets-check.html

cars travel. Each time, he arrives at 5% or less as the amount of time cars are actually in use.[22]

The good news is that the newer technologies can actually make the world more accessible to everyone. However, there is a lot of work to do to assure access for everyone.

> *"Uber has incorporated accessible technology for Deaf and hard of hearing people directly into their app, providing unprecedented access for the Deaf community to make money by driving with Uber. This partnership with CSD will provide more than a simple opportunity for Deaf driver-partners to give rides to people on the road — it's an opportunity to build bridges between people and influence a new perception of the abilities and humanity of Deaf people."*[23]
>
> — Chris Soukup, CEO of the Communication Service for the Deaf

[22] http://fortune.com/2016/03/13/cars-parked-95-percent-of-time/

[23] https://accessibility.uber.com/

2

Communities

"It is also critical for brands to take the time to engage with this community and tell our stories. The reasons for this are many. There is plenty of evidence that people with disabilities are under-represented in the workforce, even though they are available and able to work. A company that shares its stories can reach out to an under-utilized talent-pool and attract such people to come and work for them, thereby improving the quality of its employee-base as a result.

In addition to the personal implications of such under-employment, there is a wider-economic impact: a company that is committed to providing productive working opportunities for people with disabilities is clearly contributing to the local and national economies in a fresh way. And of course, there's the diversity perspective – people with disabilities will inevitably have a different set of experiences and outlooks, which could be valuable insights when considering how to research and develop new products, when marketing and pitching for new busi-

ness, and of course when delivering service to a wide-demographic, and increasingly global, market."

-Steven Cox, Vice President, Fujitsu Diversity and Inclusion Ambassador - Fujitsu Global

Introduction

Communities are groups of people with common interests, similar traits or qualities. The community of persons with disabilities is unique for many reasons. We are a global community that has members from all walks of life, including economic situations, nationalities, religions, sexual orientations, and gender identities. We are the largest minority group in the world after women.

According to the World Health Organization (WHO), one in seven individuals in the world has a disability. Plus, according to National Organization on Disabilities (NOD), one in five people in the U.S. identify as having a disability under the definition of the ADA. Despite the staggering numbers of the demographics, many brands ignore our community as a viable market segment. There are many reasons why this happens, but mainly it is because brands do not understand how to include our community. There are also many myths and misunderstandings about the capabilities of this market segment.

Communities

The community of persons with disabilities also has a critical role to play to assure that brands take us seriously, and your brand can use an understanding of our efforts and struggles in this area to move this agenda forward, which in turn increases your social impact, expands your customer base and benefits your bottom line.

We have struggled with our global identity for many years. We break into smaller groups instead of pulling together to create a stronger cohesive voice. When I speak to the community of persons with disabilities, I encourage us to break down the silos and barriers we have created within our community. We need to unite together to help solve many of our **common struggles**. **These efforts** will help unite individuals in our community and can create a sense of urgency to assure inclusion and accessibility.

We will discuss the opportunities for both corporate brands and the community of persons with disabilities to work together to make the world a better place for everyone. Society would function better if these two communities came together and learned how to fully include individuals with disabilities in their workforces and client bases. Brands would benefit by having loyal customers, and the community would win by supporting brands that support us.

A Global Breakthrough in Understanding Disability

A remarkable development occurred in 2006 when, after several years of negotiations, the United Nations completed the drafting of the Convention of the Rights for Persons with Disabilities (CRPD, also known in the disability field as The Convention). Its impact is considerable: Ten years later, 161 countries had ratified it, establishing the foundation for disability rights in many countries that did not have any disability policy or legislation.

The CRPD is based on a social model for disability. It defines persons with disabilities as including *"those who have long-term physical, mental, intellectual, or sensory impairments which in interaction with various barriers may hinder their full and effective participation in society on an equal basis with others."*[24]

The CRPD thus defines disability as the consequence of the interaction between an impairment that may be mental, cognitive, physical, sensory, emotional, developmental, or a combination of these, and social and environmental barriers.

It promotes a **social model of disability** as opposed to the older **medical model of disability**. The social model of disability identifies systemic barriers, negative attitudes, and exclusion caused by society (purposely or inadvertently), indicating that society is the main contributory factor in disabling people. Physical, sensory, intellectual, or psychological variations may cause

[24] Convention on the Rights of Persons with Disabilities, Art.1

individual functional limitation or impairments, but persons with disabilities can be meaningfully included in society unless society fails to take account of and include people regardless of their individual differences.

Also important is the language used to discuss those with disabilities. **People-focused language** or **people-first language** always puts the person before the disability. Instead of "disabled people," "disabled employees," or "blind person," it is more appropriate to say "persons with disabilities," "employees with disabilities," "person who is blind." This prevents people from feeling like they are only a label.

An Evolving Perception among Businesses

Businesses' perspectives on the scope of the community of persons with disabilities have evolved as demographics have become more comprehensive. For many years in the United States – and still today in many countries – census methodologies minimized the actual numbers of persons with disabilities by utilizing medical types of questions that most people did not respond to accurately. However, recent data collection utilizing functional definitions (things that people can or cannot do in their everyday life) rather than medical definitions have vastly expanded the breadth and depth of data available. Those new census data also give a more realistic assessment of the number of persons living with disabilities.

As a result, companies all around the world recognize the imperative to develop their capacity to market and serve persons with disabilities, senior citizens in particular. Not surprisingly, businesses in fast aging countries such as Japan or Italy tend to be more focused on those issues than others. In the mobile marketplace, for instance, NTT DoCoMo, the leading Japanese operator pioneered its "Raku-Raku" mobile product line for persons with disabilities and seniors. By tailoring its products and services to different types of impairment, it acquired more than 20 million new clients since the inception of the product line[25]. Similarly, banks in the United States, Canada and the United Kingdom such as Barclays Bank, TD Bank, Wells Fargo, and JP Morgan Chase have ramped up their services for the community of persons with disabilities including seniors.

The bottom line is that companies are increasingly aware of the imperative to address this major global segment of the population. Companies also realize that they are more competitive and better positioned to meet this objective if their workforce reflects their marketplace.

Brand Reputation

A brand's reputation can be enhanced by ensuring everyone is included in the workforce and client base. Hiring persons with disabilities has many bottom-line benefits. It is not only about persons with disabilities, but it is also about their families and friends, as well as social good. It is also good for the brand to be perceived as an exemplary employer, exemplary neighbor, and exemplary company with innovative solutions.

---

[25] NTT DoCoMo presentation at the 2014 M-Enabling Summit

Communities

Many people are surprised to learn just how much of the world's population is affected by a disability, and how valuable an accessible environment is to the workforce and to the global marketplace. Disabilities are a normal part of life: One may be born with a disability or acquire it during his or her lifetime after an accident, health issue, act of war, natural disaster, or as a result of aging. Persons with disabilities are not broken, they are like everyone else; they just have to navigate the world in a different way.

Different cultures, religions, and countries define disability differently. These different definitions can be confusing to all stakeholders, including the community of persons with disabilities, governments, associations, multinational companies, and organizations trying to support the community. An example of this confusion is the situation of little people. In some countries, like the United States, little people are covered in definitions, but in other countries, they are not. A similar situation exists for those with mental health impairments; differing definitions, inclusions, and exclusions result in these people holding different status in different countries.

As your brand evolves in your perceptions of persons with disabilities you gain the opportunity to set an example, not just for your customer base, but also for your customers with disabilities in nations that do not recognize them in beneficial ways and for those nations themselves. In this way, you can position yourself as a leader in the area of inclusivity and forge an exemplary reputation.

Brands like Barclays Bank in the UK are embracing all segments of the community. It is encouraging to see this international bank understanding the value of full inclusion of all customers and employees.

"Many organisations are waking up to the fact that leaning in and embracing accessibility and an inclusive design mindset leads to multiple benefits – reducing legal risks, strengthening brand, improving customer experience and colleague productivity.

When we shift our thinking beyond minimum legal compliance and instead to the commercial opportunity and creative challenge that arises from building better experiences for the broadest customer base, it's simply good for business and good for society.

At Barclays, we've been working hard to shift our colleague culture from perceiving accessibility from something that legally we have to do to instead something that commercially and morally we want to do. We've built awareness, know-how, empathy and champions from searching out and telling those stories of customers with access needs who have both positive experiences as well as bad ones – this humanises the conversation and shows the difference that thoughtful, inclusive design can have.

By aiming to inspire hearts, educate heads and enable hands of our colleagues to really buy into and cham-

pion the agenda within the bank, this is now starting to shine through externally to the communities that we serve and the customer interactions that we have. Colleagues are proud of what we've achieved to date and energised to actively listen and engage with customers with access needs to do more.

I've also been humbled to review much of the positive customer feedback we receive as well as noting how influential customers with disabilities can be – from influencing their household spending decisions on accessible retailors or restaurants to singing the praises of these same brands to their sizeable social media communities. We've shared our accessibility journey and useful resources on our Accessibility B2B website, and we've seen a significant increase in interest from suppliers or organisations who bank with us wanting to learn and do more in this space themselves. The fact we have a publicly stated ambition to become the most accessible FTSE company in the UK also re-enforces that this is something we're serious about thanks to top-down support and sponsorship from our Barclays executives."

-Paul Smyth, head of Digital Accessibility, Barclays

Disability Inclusion and Accessibility

Businesses work hard to create positive brand recognition. Brands who include persons with disabilities among their employees create an excellent way to enhance brand image. Persons with disabilities should be viewed as a viable pool of potential employees as well as an emerging market that, together with their friends, families, and caregivers, have trillions of dollars in disposable income. Stories of successful disability inclusion within a company should be included in marketing efforts, shareholder reports, and corporate social responsibility reports.

Advocates supportive of these inclusive efforts have used various communication channels to encourage the community of persons with disabilities to reward brands by 'voting with our wallets.' We also write letters to the CEO's and Board of Directors thanking them for including us, and with strategic encouragement from brands, more of this is possible.

The Facts: Latest Demographics

As stated earlier in this chapter, the 2011 World Health Organization (WHO) report, one out of seven people—approximately 15 percent of the world's populations—have a disability. That is over a billion people. Nearly two hundred million of these people with disabilities have severe difficulties in functioning.

Looking at the stats from the US lens we find that the percentage of people with disabilities is larger than any single ethnic, racial, or cultural group. In the United States, at 19.3 percent, the number of people with disabilities exceeds the next largest minority group—Hispanic people (14.9 percent) —by a fairly wide margin.[26] According to the National Organization on Disabilities, one out of three US households is impacted by disabilities.[27]

Looking at the numbers from a global perspective really shows the power of this community. Here are some statistics from World Health Organization:

Global Disability Stats

More than one billion people or about 15% of the world's population live with disabilities – that's 1 in 7 people. In the United States, 1 in 5 people identifies as having a disability.

Canada	3.8 Million
Australia	4 Million
	1 in 5 people
Japan	5 Million
	127.8 are elderly
UK	8.6 Million
Russia	13 – 15 Million
Europe	39 Million
Latin America & Caribbean	50 Million
Middle East	50 Million
China	60 Million
	130M+ over 60
United States	60 Million
	1 in 3 households impacted
Africa	80 Million

26 http://www.ada.gov/buisstat.htm_(date accessed 02/22/2015)

27 http://serviceandinclusion.org/index.php?page=basic (date accessed 02/22/2015)

India 40 – 80 Million

Statistics Source - World Health Organization

Aging

Aging societies are an important part of the conversation and demographics. As societies age, more people will acquire disabilities. There is a global increase in chronic health conditions like cancer, diabetes, cardiovascular disease, and mental health disorders. This is particularly true in countries like Japan, Canada, and the United States, where people between ages fifty and sixty-nine— born between the years 1946 and 1964—are often referred to as "baby boomers." "The last of the baby boomers turned 50 in 2014, and there are currently over 100 million adults in the United States over the age of 50." [28]

The population over age sixty-five is expected to rise from 15.5 percent of the EU population in 1995 to 22.4 percent by 2025.[29]

- Those over fifty years of age currently account for one-fifth of the UK population. Surprising to some, 33 percent of fifty- to sixty-year-olds now have a disability.[30]

[28] https://www.immersionactive.com/item/stats-facts/

[29] http://www.boston-ia.org/library/presentations/gribbons_presentation_2005.html (date accessed 02/22/2015)

[30] http://www.slideshare.net/NordeaBank/nordea-csr-report-2013 (date accessed 02/22/2015)

- Many think of disabilities in extreme terms such as blindness and deafness, but it also includes others with visual or hearing impairments, along with such challenges as motor and cognitive impairment, which are increasingly common in our aging population.

United States Census Bureau Disability Statistics[31]

The Census Bureau breaks down data by disability type. Despite this data being US-based, it can be used as an indicator of how disabilities statistics break down globally.

U.S. Census Bureau American Community Survey

Prevalence of Disability for Selected Age Groups: 2005 and 2010 (Shown below as a percentage of total population)

All Ages:	**2005**	**2010**
With a disability	18.7	18.7
Severe disability	12.0	12.6
Aged 6 and older		
Needed personal assistance	4.1	4.4
Aged 15 and older		
With a disability	21.3	21.3
Severe Disability	14.2	14.8
Difficulty Seeing	3.4	3.3

31 http://www.census.gov/people/disability/publications/sipp2010.html

Severely Vision Impaired		0.8	0.8
Difficulty Hearing		3.4	3.1
Severely Hearing Impaired		0.4	0.5
Aged 21 – 64			
With a disability		16.5	16.6
Employed	45.6	41.1	
Severe Disability		11.0	11.4
Employed	30.7	27.5	
Non-severe disability		5.5	5.2
Employed	75.2	71.2	
No disability		83.5	83.4
Employed	83.5	79.1	
Aged 65 and older			
With a disability		51.8	49.8
Severe Disability		36.9	36.6

Community of Persons with Disabilities Finds Our Voice

Speaking to the community of persons with disabilities is always a treat for me since I am part of the community. In part due to my encouragement and that of other leaders in our community, and in part due to the natural evolution of consumerism, the community of persons with disabilities is starting to support the corporate brands that support us, making a win/win for us all. Our efforts are leading to better employment outcomes and options for the community of persons with disabilities around the world, and full inclusion of a diverse workforce that includes individuals with disabilities has become an important part of a company's identity.

The community is joining social media and other community conversations in greater numbers and coming to understand which brands are trying to include us. We are increasingly buying products and services from inclusive brands and letting you know that we appreciate your inclusion efforts. In this way, we are becoming loyal champions for the brands that include us. We are writing letters to CEOs and Boards of Directors and tagging inclusive brands on social media to thank you for your efforts. As members of the community of persons with disabilities, we are encouraging our employers to hire and retain persons with disabilities, setting up employee resource groups, encouraging them to become accessible to employees and customers, and applauding efforts to include models with visible disabilities in your marketing efforts.

In increasing numbers, we are coming to understand the benefit of expecting that brands get a positive Return on Investment (ROI) for your efforts. The critical understanding that this is NOT about 'The Right Thing to Do" is replacing the naïve notion that corporations should not make money through their inclusive efforts. That's why you are in business: to make money. Instead, this is about changing the world to assure that everyone has a place to contribute and work and that we as a community know which brands are trying to be holistic. If inclusive companies do not make money by creating products and services that include our community, then we all fail.

We are striving to help corporate brands understand that this is no longer about charity. For example, US corporate engagement with our community is now all about ROI and increased shareholder value. We are helping corporate brands understand that any measure pursued to streamline your process for improved accessibility within your workforce directly affects increased productivity to ALL your employees and customers with and without disabilities, as detailed in my book Tapping into Hidden Human Capital. This increased productivity equates to real Corp ROI, resulting in better competitiveness to the industry and larger returns to the shareholders.

Runway of Dreams Foundation and Tommy Hilfiger Brand

Let's look at an example of a corporate brand that is working hard to reach out to the community of persons with disabilities. Tommy Hilfiger Brand[32] supports the community of persons with disabilities in many ways. One of the most exciting is the partnership between Tommy Hilfiger and Runway of Dreams Foundation (RODF).

Based upon the initial success of the line, the company now plans to expand this effort to adults and help the rest of the fashion industry understand the win for everyone. They also have clothes at all price points, and it helps draw people to their brands as well as other companies that are supporting this community so that they can support them in return.

Runway of Dreams Foundation Founding Story

Runway of Dreams Foundation (RODF)[33] was founded in 2014 by Mindy Scheier - a fashion designer and mother of a child with a disability. After graduating from the University of Vermont, Mindy spent over 20 years working in fashion as a key member of the design team for the INC collection and stylist for Saks Fifth Avenue in New York City. Her career path took a new direction when her son Oliver, who has a rare form of Muscular Dystrophy, wanted to wear jeans to school like his friends.

---

32 http://usa.tommy.com/en/runway-of-dreams

33 http://runwayofdreams.org/home/

She soon realized that millions of people around the world were also struggling to access fashionable clothing that meets their needs and began to develop modifications — including closures, adjustments and alternative ways in and out of the clothing — to meet a wide variety of needs within the differently-abled community. She envisioned a world where adaptive clothing for people with disabilities was mainstream.

After spending 20 years in the fashion industry and opening a design school for kids, Mindy decided to combine her experience and her passion by creating the Runway of Dreams Foundation, a nonprofit that works to broaden the reach of adaptive clothing and promote people with disabilities in fashion through inclusion, empowerment, and opportunity.

Today, Mindy continues to break down barriers and challenge industry norms. The need for inclusion and accessibility for the differently-abled community in fashion goes beyond adaptive clothing. The Runway of Dreams Foundation works on multiple fronts to develop, deliver and support initiatives to broaden the reach of adaptive clothing and promote the differently-abled community in the fashion industry. Through adaptive clothing donations, employment opportunity initiatives, adaptive design workshops, awareness building campaigns and scholarships programs, the Runway of Dreams Foundation is empowering people with disabilities with opportunity, confidence, independence, and style.

Runway of Dreams Foundation Pillars

The Runway of Dreams Foundation relies on three pillars in its mission to broaden the reach of adaptive clothing and promote people with disabilities in fashion. These are inclusion, empowerment, and opportunity.

- INCLUSION: Disability affects people of all ages, races, ethnicities and socioeconomic backgrounds. To make fashion truly accessible and inclusive for all, the Runway of Dreams Foundation increases access to mainstream adaptive clothing through donations and clothing grants.

- EMPOWERMENT: The Runway of Dreams Foundation facilitates community building between the fashion industry and differently-abled community to celebrate people's differences and break down stereotypes. Through ambassador programs, storytelling campaigns and community-driven initiatives, the Runway of Dreams Foundation empowers and connects people of all abilities around the belief that fashion inspires confidence, independence, and self-expression.

- OPPORTUNITY: The Runway of Dreams Foundation creates opportunities within the fashion industry for people with disabilities and for those working to broaden the reach of adaptive fashion design. From workshops and symposiums to adaptive design scholarships and modeling gigs, the Runway of Dreams Foundation is increasing representation through opportunity.

Additional resources can be found at:

https://www.youtube.com/watch?v=-hLlSgiv0_c&t=78s

https://www.youtube.com/watch?v=riZPN8WAcEM

https://www.youtube.com/watch?v=GSuVGwDb6bs

https://mic.com/articles/185790/meet-mindy-scheier-the-mom-fighting-to-make-clothes-for-people-with-disabilities-mainstream#.50LA5LjDo

http://www.womansday.com/life/inspirational-stories/a60551/halloween-for-kids-with-disabilities/

3

Creating Engagement

"At Accenture, we believe that diversity makes us stronger, smarter and more innovative. Each person has unique skills, talent, and strengths, and there should be no barrier to opportunities because of a disability – whether hidden or visible. In the past couple of years, we have moved from sharing this commitment among our people and stakeholders to taking measurable actions to ensure an inclusive environment where people of all abilities can thrive.

Our focus has been on taking a hard look at our systems and processes to ensure accessibility internally and partnering with companies like Microsoft and SAP for best practices along the way. One way we get feedback on how we are doing is by participating in external rankings, including the Disability Equality Index and the National Organization on Disability's Leading Employer Seal. Our ambition is to be the most inclusive employer in the world. We still have work to do and will continue to push ourselves through the lens of accommodations, accessibility, attitudinal changes, and accountability."

-Daniel Ellerman, senior manager – Human Resources and Global Persons with Disabilities Program Lead

Introduction

Engaging with customers and communities on social media can be interesting at best and sometimes downright scary. Is the brand using the right terminology? Are you being empathic and understanding? How should brands engage with audiences in authentic ways that drive brand loyalty? We will discuss these topics and more in this chapter. We will also look at ways to humanize your brand. Many brands do not effectively engage on social media because they are afraid to make mistakes. That is a missed business opportunity. We will explore ways to meaningfully engage with the community of individuals with disabilities. These tips can also be used for other communities, to engage with your clients and other audience members.

Humanizing the Brand - Transformation

Social media can help humanize your brand. It is a powerful way to provide visual storytelling to help transform an audience's impression of your brand. It is no longer traditional media versus organic media versus social media. It is all about the perception of consumers that decide what defines a business. A mcm on Facebook can redefine a brand for an entire community. That is how social media has the power to enhance the image of the brand, give it new life, and transform the brand in ways that go way beyond the initial expectation of one advertising campaign.

Companies must harness the "inside-out" model, where employees are living the right message and taking it to the world through who they are and what they do. When the employees represent diversity, inclusion, range of visible and invisible disabilities, there is authenticity in actions. This is a big deal that still makes many brands scratch their heads.

A few years ago, during a visit to the Apple store, we were talking about the accessibility of their products and how those efforts had brought tremendous value to the community of people with disabilities. Apple has set the bar high by assuring all of their products like iPhones, iPads, and Macs are very accessible. The Apple staff were proud because they have parents and individuals with disabilities coming in all the time to tell them how they're using this technology to really improve their lives.

There's beauty in technology, and for persons with certain types of disabilities, technology can be a lifeline. For example, thanks to technology the danger for persons with intellectual disabilities to become isolated due to having far fewer social opportunities than their peers is diminished. This is also happening to senior citizens. Including others means we all gain more from our increased human interaction at the same time as it means improved lives. This is why it is important for brands to clearly understand that including persons with disabilities into your workforce gives your brand insight that can only improve your final products and services, and these can then affect the lives of many.

Good for Business

Most brands genuinely want to do the right thing when it comes to the disabilities community. That's why our community must move beyond embarrassing brands to get them to include our community, and you can help this advancement along by letting us know how you are working to include us. Many representatives for large brands start the conversation with an apology: i.e., "We have not done enough to include persons with disabilities." It is a work in progress and companies need to start by celebrating current efforts and then build upon those successes. Adopting an "us" versus "them" mentality causes everyone to lose.

Many U.S. brands finally understand that "this" isn't going away. You have realized that there's legislation, litigation, brand pressure — the reality is your brand has to figure out, in an empowering way, how to include people with disabilities. Your leadership teams have also come to realize that if you don't tell your stories, somebody else might...in a very bad way.

A lot of money is being spent in this space that isn't producing positive outcomes. Brands are trying to figure out how you can best work with our community and how you can best tell your stories in a way that is empowering to us and you. And in return, our community is taking on some level of obligation as consumers to reward the brands that are trying.

Engagement

Engagement can be a powerful way to engage with clients and potential customers and an excellent way to build a community of fans that are loyal to your brand. Social media allows a corporate brand to connect one-on-one with customers, which humanizes your brand and helps you understand what your clients like, dislike, love and sometimes hate about your products, services, and customer support. Still, many brands forget or shy away from engaging with their audience, and the bottom line is that social media marketing is ineffective without engagement.

Brands need to engage with your audience so that we comment, like, and share your posts. This starts with providing content that interests, inspires, entertains and intrigues us. Then you must interact with us, listening and learning from our feedback. A negative comment can be turned into a positive experience, especially if a customer feels you are listening to their concerns. Other audience members will watch to see how you respond to the negative comments. Your response can keep the audience engaged and help build trust of your brand.

Interview with Ekaterina Walter

I had the pleasure to interview Ekaterina Walter[34]*, a globally recognized business and marketing innovator, international speaker, an author of the Wall Street Journal bestseller "Think Like Zuck" and co-author of "The Power of Visual Storytelling."*

Ekaterina[35] *discusses the importance of brand storytelling for increased profitability and social impact, and how organizations can humanize their brand through storytelling.*

Ekaterina: Social media and digital transformation as a marketer is a big thing for me. Especially, when you talk about brand storytelling. In an environment now where we live in the "age of infobicity," how do brands really stand out? The way to do it is through relating back to people's values and interests, and storytelling is one of those that fits quite naturally. Then you always have the parenting side and other passions that you have. For me, it's writing, whether it's books or articles. I always prefer to think of each person as multidimensional, and it doesn't necessarily mean just us as a professional, or us as a person. It's just one person that encompasses a variety of different things and passions and achievements that we want to accomplish in our lives, right?

---

[34] http://www.ruhglobal.com/humanizing-your-brand/
[35] http://www.ekaterinawalter.com/

Debra: Yeah, well said and we talk a lot on this program about really looking at the entire human. I know we were talking, before the show started, about your beautiful accent and your name. Tell our guests more about where you grew up.

Ekaterina: Well, I grew up in Russia, and I came to the U.S. in my early twenties. I have always been a global citizen if you will, and I've had an opportunity to work in global companies that allowed me to connect to people around the world- whether it's Europe, Asia, Latin America, or beyond. That's always been a fun thing for me, and I don't know whether it was because I was an immigrant and I had the privilege to experience living in several different countries, or whether I just feel naturally that the world is so small. And, you know, with digital and social it's getting even smaller. To me, I think people are people everywhere. No matter where we grew up, what our beliefs are, we're all humans. Connecting with folks around the world has always been a very natural thing for me. I'm really pretty privileged to have an international background and experience.

Debra: And I agree. I also do a lot of international traveling. I grew up in the United States- in Florida and then moved to Virginia, so I've lived mainly on the east coast of the United States, but I travel frequently. I just got back from the UAE, and I was having some conversations over there. I was speaking at a conference about the inclusion of people in that region with disabilities and employment and education and society at large- overall I should say- and what I find over and over again is that people are people. Parents are parents- they want the right thing for their children. They want them to have opportunities. They want the right things for their families, no matter where I go. I have actually not visited Russia yet (I hope to in the future) but I am, like you, very well traveled and I find that people are people and I think that we all want to do our best.

I agree with you also- social media has just broken down a lot of barriers. Of course, sometimes, there are people misbehaving on social media, and we've talked about that. But I love social media and the power of it, and I know you've spent quite a bit of time talking about really the power of visual storytelling and using social media to talk about not only marketing your brand from a corporate perspective but your personal and professional brand. I know you had talked about that a little bit, once again, before we started the interview. I read an article the other day that said, "Don't even bother with your personal brand. It doesn't matter anymore." I thought, "What?" I don't know that I agree with that because what is the difference between our personal brands and our professional brands?

Ekaterina: Totally. You know, it's interesting when that perspective comes up. [laughs] When the internet exploded, people started to draw attention to their content by saying, "Well the internet is dead." Then there was traditional media versus organic and social media: "Traditional media is dead." It feels to me that people seem to like to radicalize if you will, their points of view. I absolutely agree with you that the brand, whether its personal brand or corporate brand, is becoming more and more critical and more and more important. As a matter of fact, if you really look at how companies and corporations approach branding, those companies realized, finally!!!

The brands have found that they cannot hold onto their control anymore. They are not the ones who create their brand; their customers do- the people around them who have a perception of what their brand is, right? Your brand is what people say behind your back, and that's what your brand is. No matter how big your marketing department or PR department is. You can try all you want, but over 90% of content about your brand online is created by third-party sources by your clients; by your employees, et cetera.

Many corporations realized their employees can create, build, nurture, and extend their brands? And by definition, their brand will be extended through them. I am seeing (there are a few) some really smart companies taking the employees who are well known in their industry, who would like to write or speak on behalf of the company, and giving them a platform and giving them the voice.

If an employee is known for expertise on a specific subject that you have in that industry, the more value you add for your content and through your presence and through your social networks and communities that you build on social networks.

There is good statistics that show if a brand shares particular news about themselves and then an employee shares the same thing, the reach and the engagement with the employee share on their own personal networks will be 8, 10, 15 times that of the brand share, right?

Debra: So true. I know that the other day I posted a post about getting a new thermostat- a thermostat I could actually use by myself. It was made by Honeywell, and I talked about this story about my husband and I fussing with each other because neither one of us could really use our old thermostat without pulling the manual out.

It was very frustrating and the attention that story got certainly caught the eye of Honeywell. And I think that in some ways it was a more credible story coming from me than if it came from Honeywell themselves because I'm a consumer that bought their product, that really enjoyed it, and it actually was sort of funny how it added value in my home.

I agree with you, also - corporations are made of individuals, and individuals care about a lot of different things. Of course, I personally as a parent of an adult child with disabilities, I really care about disabilities, and I advocate for that all the time. And when I worked for very large banks, when I was an employee years ago, it was always something I was very passionate about, and I was always volunteering. If they were doing a United Way campaign or Easterseals or anything like that, I was always wanting to contribute to that because it was something I was very passionate about.

Corporations that are really tapping into employees to humanize their brand, I think, are very smart. And I also agree with you that not all brands are figuring that out. I've actually seen brands tell their employees not to be on social media and I think that's a huge mistake, but I think that is going away because the reality is- social media is here.

Ekaterina: You know, we talk about the fact that the companies are individuals who really make an impact, right? Whatever that impact might be. No matter if it's small or large. And I think the way to make an impact is to add value. I believe in it so much.

That's how I build large communities on social networks around me. That's how I build large networks. That is how I built some of the best relationships I've ever had in life, whether they're personal or professional. When we talk about making an impact, (and that's what I know your show is focused on) the reality is, if we don't add value, whether we're people or corporations, we're not going to be considered full-fledged contributors to society, right? And nowadays, especially when you look at the millennials, people have a high B.S. radar.

They can see through the veil, if you will, that you are trying to create if there is no truth behind it. If I look at myself as an individual, when people ask me, "How did you achieve what you have achieved?" and I say, "Look, you don't set off achieving something very specific." I guess you can always have that as your goal. The reality is, the way you grow those communities around you and the way you start making impact is you just help somebody out. Somebody asks for help; you help out. You mentor people around you. You really create content that helps other people understand what you've done and not make those mistakes. Again, whether it's in the professional world or the personal world. I've been creating for ten plus years. I've been creating content and speaking on the topics such as, "Look, I've been there, done that" and "Here's where I fell on my face- don't do that."

Here's what's happening with companies overall: the reality is, especially in the United States, over 90% of the companies compete purely on customer service. Right? If you think your product is the best out there and really going to help you continue to be a leader a decade from now, then you are absolutely mistaken. Anything can be copied within weeks, months, within a year if your product is really complex. It's not about your product. It's about those experiences you are creating for your customers.

It is about the storytelling, the bigger the amount of information that is out there, the more people really want to connect to your stories- who you are, what's going on with your company, what is happening behind-the-scenes, if your employees love you. And that's where the whole thing comes together. That sort of brand perception that you want to shape is being shaped by all of this- how you tell those stories. Do you allow your employees to tell those stories? Are they happy? Or are they not happy doing work for you? How do people relate to you? Your product? Your content that you're putting out there? Is your content promotional? Is it valuable? Right? And all of that transcends all of those boundaries and comes back to one thing: building relationship capital. And you can't build relationship capital if you're not adding value.

When you actually come in and have meaningful conversation, whether someone has trouble or an issue and you help them solve it, or somebody is really advocating for you, and you know that they're there and you go, and you thank them.

My idea on engagement is just that- you are not a brand, you are another relationship to your consumers, and if you don't really engage them, then you don't have a relationship. If the only time you're forced to engage with them is when they call your 800 number to complain about their issue, that is not engagement. Engagement is reaching out proactively and joining those conversations, whatever channels that they have.

Debra: If you are a global corporation, right, there's so many channels, and there's so many conversations that you need to listen for- you need to reach out to. That proactive approach is unfamiliar to brands. Either they're afraid, or they're just not dedicating their resources to being included in those types of conversations.

My answer to you: the brands that don't engage have no prospects for really truly building that relationship capital that will pay dividends long-term down the road. Because if you're totally quiet on me and I've been mentioning you, and I've been reaching out and giving you an opportunity to respond, and you're not there- then you don't exist. Then I'm just going to switch to your competitor because let's face it, the consumers have choices.

I really like the word you use, "relationship capital," because I have always been about relationships and one thing I'm really trying to encourage my community to do is really tap into those relationships. Once again, reward the brands that are rewarding us if a brand is working really hard to make sure people are included.

Community Expectations

Brands want consumers to do business with them because they believe in their products and services. Consumers want to trust the brands to which they show loyalty and believe that these brands are making a difference in their communities. Often the communities that brands are trying to attract do not know which brands to trust.

Target[36] has made an effort to include models with disabilities in their advertising. During a Halloween Ad Campaign, Target included a young girl with crutches modeling a Frozen costume.[37] According to their website, the ad went viral because a mother praised Target on her Facebook page. Jen Spickenagel Kroll is a mother from Michigan with a daughter who has special needs. Jen posted this comment on her Facebook page[38] in praise of Target:

> *"Dear Target, I love you. Thank you for including a child with braces and arm crutches into your advertising campaign! And as Elsa, no less! My daughter (with arm crutches and prosthetic legs) is going to FLIP when she sees this! Including children with special needs into advertising makes them less of a spectacle to the general public when they venture out into the real world. Normalizing disabilities in children is PRICELESS."*

That post has since been shared more than 8,000 times.

---

[36] www.target.com

[37] http://people.com/bodies/target-ad-shows-girl-with-disabilities-in-halloween-costume/

[38] https://www.facebook.com/jen.kroll1?fref=nf

The good news is that Target did not stop with this one ad. The company has created ads that feature child models with Down syndrome, children using a walker or a cane, children that have obvious disabilities, which is important in a visual advertisement. Remember, many people have invisible disabilities, and these are important visual cues. Consumers can look at these advertisements and immediately understand that Target intended to include the community of persons with disabilities.

There is still quite a bit of fear, with brands and the agencies that are supporting brands, of not really understanding how to talk to the community in a way that feels empowering. Likely this is the result of backlash from poor corporate attempts that result in "inspirational porn" (defined on Wikipedia as "the calling of people with disabilities inspirational solely or in part on the basis of their disability"), coined in 2012 by disability rights activist Stella Young in an editorial in Australian Broadcasting Corporation's webzine Ramp Up.[39]

Often corporate brands and your advertising and public relations firm partners do not take the time to understand the target market. When the advertisements are done incorrectly, they can actually do more harm to the brand's reputation. Remember the example of Chris Horwang talking about her career and how her white skin helped her to be so successful? When the advertisements or marketing campaigns are done thoughtfully and inclusively, however, magic can happen.

---

[39] https://en.wikipedia.org/wiki/Inspiration_porn

Live It

A growing number of corporations are really making inclusion part of your brands. Many of the leading brands have the buy-in of the executive team at the very top including the Boardroom and C-suite. Some are reaching out to other companies to help you understand how to successfully include persons with disabilities and helping other corporations also create these culture shifts.

Address Issues with Empathy

Customers are bringing issues to social media more now than ever before. Address the issues quickly and respond with empathy, take the time to answer the question and ask the customer to take it offline by Direct Messaging (DM) you.

Do not fight customers or naysayers on social media. Ever hear the advice, "Don't feed the trolls," in reference to social media? Your brand will always lose when someone is looking for a fight and being negative.

Respond to real problems, trying to offer solutions. If it gets negative and volatile come up with a strategic communications plan. You can't ignore the situation. You must have a plan.

Promote Your Brand Enthusiasts

If you have followers that are loyal to your brand called Brand Enthusiasts or Ambassadors, show them you care by retweeting, requoting, reposting and liking their comments.

I really like when a brand tweets like '@debraruh Thank you for Flying @Delta we appreciate your business' or '@debraruh thanks for your tweet - We are glad you like your service today at @BestBuy. Some brands even allow the social media team to personalize the tweet: '@debraruh thanks for your kind words about @buffer. We appreciate you. Kim.'

It is also okay to ask customers to @mention you or use a carefully selected hashtag. Be sure your social media team does their homework. You do not want to use a hashtag for a big campaign that was used for things that could embarrass your brand. It has happened!!!

Use social media to get people excited about the new release. Tease them with a few new details, and then encourage them to click to your website to learn more.

Follow Back

Social media is social. Most brands think it is a one-sided conversation – you tell us why we need to be your customer and we just hold on to your every word. Nope, not anymore, and it is sad to say most brands only follow back your teams and partners, or there seems to be no plan at all.

Brands are not expected to follow every single person back, but have a strategic plan for following.

Remember that your followers can only see your tweets, not your followers' tweets, so there is no harm in following back, and it sure impresses your customers and potential customers.

Many users will unfollow you even if you are a brand, (I do), if you do not follow back. Also, remember that some social media platforms like Twitter have an algorithm of followers versus following.

I will be honest here – most brands do not follow users back. Want to stick with the pack – do not follow us pesky customers. Want to be a brand that engages with your audience? Follow us and join the conversations.

WARNING: Do not BUY Followers – some high profile social media leaders have lost millions of followers overnight. WHY? Because they paid for fake followers. Makes your numbers look good, BUT it is very embarrassing to lose that many followers overnight when the social media platforms purge the fake accounts. Earn your followers the old-fashioned way – engage and provide good content and FOLLOW BACK.

Otherwise, think of how it looks to your customers. It looks like you think you deserve an audience member to follow you, but they do not have anything of value to say to you. Millennials really hate that behavior. Not only is it a mistake, but you will lose followers when you do not follow back.

Now if a social media user is misbehaving on social media, it's okay to not follow them or to stop following them. I have over 170,000 followers on Twitter as of this writing, and I follow about 95% of them back.

Use Hashtags

Use all your social media tools, and remember that hashtags are a powerful tool. Hashtags allow a brand to reach audiences that are tracking certain topics. Research the hashtags in your industry. For example, I track #disabilities, #inclusion, #AXSChat, #ChangeAgents, #PinkSocks, #Women4Women, #SDGs, #TuesdayGiving and other hashtags that are focused on social good.

There are free tools that rate the effectiveness of one hashtag over another. One example is https://ritetag.com/

Once you select the hashtags, track the conversations and the top leaders of that hashtag, and then carefully join the conversations. You can also join tweet chats like #AXSChat to listen to the community.

The good news on social media is that you can read and review hashtags or tweet chats without anyone knowing you are monitoring them, just to get your feet wet before joining the conversations.

Rewards

We all love getting free prizes and winning contests even small silly ones. We also like getting bling with your brand on it. I remember when Buffer sent me a package of goodies. Stickers, a pen, and some other small things. I really appreciated it. I took a picture of the bling and my daughter and posted it on Twitter. It was retweeted over 200+ times. Good marketing and I like my little prizes. I was already a fan of Buffer but now feel even more loyal to them.

Spark intrigue among your audience by offering the freebies, shout-out for best tweet of the day about your product or other creative ways to reward your social media followers. Remember the Buffer story. We all love bling.

Follow the example of reward clubs like the hotels or airlines. Rewards do not always have to have monetary value. A shout-out of social media is powerful. Example: @debraruh good job on your webinar last week #ChangeAgents

Measure

Remember to measure your social media successes. This allows you to re-share messages and can improve future content. Social media analytics can PROVE the ROI for a brand.

Look for trends within your content and social media networks. This allows a brand to understand the true engagement on social media. You can also track marketing campaigns, SEO or website spikes via your social media metrics.

Measuring engagement depends on the social media platform. They all have to be measured differently, and your social media team must learn the unique aspects of each one.

Take the time to understand what is working and compare your social media stats between platforms with tools like Buffer[40], NUVI[41], Hootsuite[42] or TweetDeck[43].

In conclusion, a brand must be on social media in this day and age. If you have the right marketing plan, a solid team, and good content, your brand can blossom on social media. I am always here to answer questions or provide guidance. Engage with the community of persons with disabilities and use that knowledge to engage with other communities. Social media can be a win-win for everyone.

40 www.Buffer.com

41 www.NUVI.com

42 www.hootsuite.com

43 https://tweetdeck.twitter.com/

4

Risks

"As businesses, our brand and our behavior are inextricably linked. In an era of disruption, our brand values may be the difference between success and failure. Those values may address perceived value or quality. But increasingly, those values will reflect perceptions of service and customer care. The ways in which we offer access and inclusion, meeting the needs of all customers, may shape those perceptions significantly."

-David Banes, Director, David Banes Access and Inclusion Services

Introduction

Living in the United States but traveling extensively globally and consulting with the United Nations has allowed me the benefit of having a bird's eye view of corporate brands interacting with the persons with disabilities community. It has not been a fun journey for many corporations trying to comply with the laws regarding disability inclusion, ICT Accessibility, and Built Barriers. These laws have been in place for more than almost 30 years, but the litigation over lack of access is now higher than ever before with the lawyers stating that they are now going to branch out from web accessibility lawsuits to inaccessible mobile apps, proxy and customer statements and privacy statements.

Of great interest to corporations is the considerable positive impact that Information and Communication Technologies (ICT), the Internet and mobile technologies can have on their interactions with persons with disabilities as employees or customers.

This is an exciting time, with emerging new technologies and mobile computing devices enabling people of all ages and all levels of education to communicate, access information, manage their environment through the internet of things (IoT) with alternate modes of communications such as speech recognition, biometrics or text to speech embedded in most smartphones and tablets.

These developments open opportunities for persons with disabilities to join the workforce and help create innovative processes and solutions for their employers. Designing and delivering ICT to be fully accessible ensures all individuals can enjoy the benefits and advantages of technology and add greater value to the workforce.

Adopting an inclusive, accessible, and universal design approach to technology is, therefore, a smart strategy for both public and private organizations wishing to proactively adjust to the future needs of this growing population. By recognizing the importance of the protection and promotion of the rights and dignity of persons with disabilities through innovative assistive technologies and accessible ICTs, corporations can better ensure the full inclusion of individuals in the workforce.

Compliance vs. Human Rights and Market Opportunities

While accessible ICTs and the Internet are great enablers, they can also present important challenges for corporations when accessibility requirements are not met. Corporations get sued for operating inaccessible websites or publishing inaccessible e-book readers. This is a global trend: in China, the United Kingdom, Australia or Hungary, advocates bring cases of inaccessible websites, telephone services, or bank ATMs to court. And in the United States, the Department of Justice is definitely increasing its pressure on large organizations to align their websites with web accessibility standards. As the following chapters will demonstrate, corporations are at the crossroads of compliance pressures, Human Rights, Citizenship considerations and market opportunities.

Benefiting from the experience and perspectives of employees and executives with disabilities has never been as important. And employing a diverse workforce inclusive of persons with disabilities creates benefits in many ways: enhanced reputation, reduction in risk, innovation opportunities, and productivity gains. And most importantly, it nurtures a loyal, productive, and innovative workforce.

Litigation

In late 2014, I started writing my book, "Uncovering Hidden Human Capital: How Leading Corporations Leverage Multiple Abilities in Their Workforce," published by G3ict in 2016.[44] At the time, I asked approximately ten U.S. based multi-national brands to be part of the best practice sections of the book. Many of the corporations came back and said, 'Debra, we would love to be featured in the book, but our legal team has said no." They were nervous about being featured in my book as demonstrating a best practice because they felt it made them a target for additional lawsuits.

I wrote a blog back in 2012 about Walt Disney Parks & Resorts called 'No Good Deed Goes Unpunished.'[45]

The blog explored the class action lawsuit back in 2011 against Walt Disney Parks & Resorts. I was perplexed with this Americans with Disability Act (ADA) lawsuit. Why the surprise? The American Foundation for the Blind (AFB) had just awarded Disney with a 2011 Access Award[46], one of the highest honors a

[44] http://tinyurl.com/hnvzswu
[45] http://www.ruhglobal.com/no-good-deed-goes-unpunished/
[46] http://afb.org/section.asp?documentid=5410

brand can get from the community of persons with disabilities in the U.S.

I am not here to debate the merits of the case, but it was confusing for Disney to win this award and then immediately get sued for violating the ADA. Are they horrible, wonderful, or maybe just trying their best?

I understand many moving parts exist when dealing with disability inclusion and accessibility. However, the litigious approach can send the wrong message to brands. When I asked major multi-national brands in the U.S. in 2014 to be part of my book, they quickly said, "no Debra we have not done enough."

It made me sad because many brands in the U.S. have been working on disability inclusion and accessibility for many years. Are they perfect? NO. Are they trying? Absolutely.

Back to my book. It took a few years to get my book completed. In early 2016, several of the U.S. brands that had declined in late 2014 came back and asked if they could be in the book. I asked them what had changed. There was a common thread in their responses: Inclusion of persons with disabilities is part of our efforts. We understand that operating in the U.S. means we may face lawsuits. It is just part of doing business in the U.S. So instead of focusing on being perfect, we want to share our stories of inclusion and accessibility with the community of persons with disabilities. By telling the stories of the brands that are working towards full inclusion, we can hopefully educate the entire ecosystem about how the great benefits of inclusion greatly outweigh the complexities.

There's got to be a way to identify what can make the sand fall faster in the hourglass. Beyond the legal challenge, past the threat of bad press, there are hot buttons that resonate with people in a company. They may be at different levels of the operation, some at the C-suite and others on the line, but using best practices from other topics that have "metrics" monitored by the business hawks, we should be able to say what will make the clock tick faster toward inclusion reality.

The Inclusion Roadmap

To ensure that your brand is successful with all the moving parts of inclusion of persons with disabilities, you need to create a roadmap to implement disability inclusion and accessibility. The inclusion roadmap helps blend accessibility into your processes, track progress and measure results. The roadmap should include a plan with deliverables, timelines, and metrics.

In fact, disability inclusion and accessibility initiatives can be risky without a plan. This is primarily because it may be subject to departmental interpretations and adjustments across diverse organizations. To be sure that the enterprise is pursuing inclusion in a legal and consistent manner, you need to put time, thought, and funding into evaluating your current practices and planning how you will adjust them.

Risks

Many organizations benefit by working with accessibility and disability inclusion strategists. A seasoned professional can help you create a solid plan of attack.

Inclusion Roadmap Ideas

Here are a few ideas to include in an inclusion roadmap:

1. **Vision/mission statement**

    a. Blend inclusion of persons with disabilities right into the inclusion roadmap's vision/mission statement.

    b. Specify that the brand is committed to full inclusion and the integration of accessible design for employees and customers. Be sure to blend this commitment into every phase of the business, including employment, product design, policies and procedures, procurement, supply chain, and every department/function (e.g., human resources, financial, operations, marketing and communications, corporate social responsibility or citizenship, and training).

    c. Try not to implement accessibility by creating separate technology or business processes; instead, mainstream accessibility and inclusion policies in all technology and business processes.

2. **Diversity programs** are often viewed as a bridge between the workplace and the marketplace.

a. When creating employment policies and programs, such as Equal Employment Opportunity or affirmative action policies in the United States, include disability, inclusion and accessibility components.

b. The programs should be owned by line management organization, in addition to human resources. Be sure to include accountability mechanisms that require reporting to the Board of Directors, CEO, chief risk or compliance officer, and human resources leaders.

3. **Recruitment policies and practices** should reflect a commitment to accessibility in this stage of employment, including the use of accessible e-recruiting tools and accommodation policies for interviews.

4. **Retention and disability inclusion management and prevention programs.** Create programs that allow employees to remain part of the workforce in the case of temporary or permanent disabilities. This allows an employer to keep experienced workers' intellectual capital and avoid retraining and the expense of replacing talented employees.

5. **Awareness and training on disability.** Expand base of knowledge and experience about disability inclusion and accessibility for all employees through various strategies such as training sessions, demonstrations, newsletters. Best results in promoting disability inclusion are obtained with required training of all employees on an annual basis. Thereby allowing this process to be a sustainable practice that then becomes a core element of the corporate culture of the company.

6. **Procurement policies.** Adopt criteria for the purchase and use of information and communication technology (ICT) that is accessible and usable; this is sometimes referred to as universal design. This policy has many benefits, to your customers assuring they have access to your services and products. It can also increase productivity, reduction in the time it takes for employees to transition between systems, reduction in training, remediation and repurposing. The policy also helps reduce risks to the firm, since it allows all employees to use the new system, product, or tools and helps comply with standards, treaties and legal requirements such as ADA and Rehabilitation Act, Section 508 in the United States or United Nations Convention on the Rights of Persons with Disabilities (CRPD).

7. **Promote the company's achievements in disability inclusion and accessibility as a "differentiator."** Applicants, employees, customers, and other stakeholders are increasingly seeking accessible information and communication technology. Showing a company commitment to disability inclusion, accessibility, and universal design standards and governance help position it as an "employer of choice," which also resonates with the general public.

8. **Supply chain policies.** Consider expanding your supplier diversity programs to include businesses that are 51 percent or more owned, operated, controlled, and managed by individual(s) with disabilities.

9. **Communication policies.** Ensure that marketing, communications, and websites are fully accessible, on both the internet and a company's intranet sites.

10. **Product development.** Build, implement, and manage accessible products and services.

11. **Telecommuting programs.** If the company has a telecommuting program, use it to accommodate schedules of employees with disabilities including the flexibility to work from home or at other remote sites away from the office, such as on the road or at a telework center.

12. **Employee resource groups or affinity group.** Establish and support an employee resource group for employees with disabilities and their families. Such networks facilitate communications between employees to share initiatives, ideas, accommodation solutions, and best practices. These groups can also help managers overcome resistance to creating accessible and inclusive business policies and practices. They can also help identify policies and practices that need to be addressed, as well as expand and improve how the company does business with its customers from a disability perspective.

13. **Designation of authority-centralized responsibility and source of information.** It will help to designate one contact point in a department whose responsibility it is to ensure consistent focus and resources are provided to employees on disability inclusion. This responsibility should include the development, implementation, and evaluation of accessibility and usability (universal design) initiatives.

14. **Cross-functional communications and coordination.** Formalize team approach (e.g., accessibility team comprised of managers across divisions such as human resources, facilities, information and communication technology, procurement, education and training, financial, and every aspect of your internal and external corporate marketing).

15. **Internships/mentoring/shadowing programs** provide equal opportunities for individuals with disabilities to participate in company programs.

Measure – Mitigate Risk

Risk mitigation remains a key concern for brands especially with allowing customers with disabilities to have the same access to services and products as other customers. This can also impact employers in relation to the employment of persons with disabilities, especially in those countries with a strong litigation culture.

The most effective way to reduce risk is to create and implement a comprehensive disability inclusion plan or roadmap as described above. While compliance should not be the driving factor to promote the inclusion of customers and employees with disabilities, it is important to make all management levels of the organization aware of the potential liabilities that can result from missteps in customer access, and the recruitment, management or termination of employees with disabilities.

5

Understand the Community and Building Brand Ambassadors

"Throughout my time here at Hewlett Packard Enterprise, I've witnessed the power of inclusion in action. As a tech company with innovation embedded deep in its DNA, it is imperative to ensure that all of our people can bring their whole self to work. There is no denying that when you foster an inclusive environment, you allow for the magic to happen – one that brings transformative ideas to life.

We all bring different points of view, shaped by our experience, background, gender, unique abilities, etc. I have always said innovation comes from all angles and from the convergence of different perspectives. Those that embrace this fact will continue to win in the marketplace."

- Jesse Cortez, Global Inclusion Effectiveness Lead at Hewlett Packard Enterprise

Understand the Community and Building Brand Ambassadors

Introduction

Every brand needs loyal brand ambassadors. This chapter will discuss ways to find, recruit, encourage, and engage with brand ambassadors (also known as brand advocates) programs as part of your marketing strategy. This can be an excellent way to engage with the community of persons with disabilities. The program allows a brand to create processes for executing activities that can help build brand awareness. When creating a program remember to create clear goals, recognition and rewards programs.

Bottom-line, it is critical for a brand to have brand ambassadors. A brand ambassador is a person who is loyal to your brand, not a paid endorser but an individual who likes or even loves your services or products. Positive comments and reviews from credible sources are critical for a brand.

Why You Need Brand Ambassadors

A survey created by SDL[47] in 2013 noted that 58% of consumers shared their positive brand experiences on social media. According to Nielsen's latest Trust In Advertising report,[48] in both "advertising via old standbys like TV, newspapers, and radio or newer media like mobile and online, earning consumer trust

47 http://www.sdl.com/about/news-media/press/2013/sdl-survey-reveals-consumers-want-brands-to-offer-consistent-experience.html
48 http://www.nielsen.com/us/en/insights/news/2013/under-the-influence-consumer-trust-in-advertising.html

is the holy grail of a successful campaign." The Nielsen report showed that 84% of the consumers polled said that they completely or somewhat trust recommendations from friends, family, and colleagues and rank those recommendations as the most trustworthy. This confirms what we already know by now, that what people say about your brand, whether negative or positive, has an impact. By equipping your marketing machine with the loyalty and support of brand ambassadors, you make the most of your power to control how your brand is perceived.

Good brand ambassadors are such a versatile and powerful branding and marketing tool because they can cut through the clutter and say things about your company and brand with more credibility than the brand can. When I praise a brand for giving me or my family good service – it is more powerful than the brand saying they have good service, as illustrated in the Honeywell example. This type of credibility is critical for direct outreach to communities like the community of persons with disabilities. And reaching this community is advantageous because people with disabilities talk about brands to their family, friends, and colleagues in everyday conversations and on social media, making them an excellent source of brand ambassadors.

Additionally, brand ambassadors are passionate enough that you can call on them repeatedly, in many different situations and have confidence that they will continue to share their great experiences with family, friends and their communities.

How to Create a Brand Ambassador Program

A brand ambassador program is a structured program utilizing loyal customers to encourage positive word-of-mouth to amplify brand awareness and gain other loyal customers. A good place to find brand ambassadors is among your loyal and happy customers, so take the time to engage with these customers. Repost, retweet and thank them, reward them with company swag and ask them why they like your brand. You can also ask them for suggestions for improving your services and products. This engagement encourages them to speak about your brand even more. Strong brand ambassadors can add a layer and texture to your existing marketing campaigns.

In addition to brand ambassadors, your brand ambassador program needs a point of engagement to help market your brand. Examples include social media, blogs, articles and community events like musical concerts, festivals, sports events, disability expos or conferences and other community activities that can help create buzz for your brand. The brand ambassadors' strength lies in their ability to influence their own audience and yours, and thereby strengthen the customer-product/service relationship. Brand ambassadors can promote, provide customer service, and act as champions for your brand.

Remember to allow the brand ambassadors to have flexibility so they can communicate the messaging in their own style, allowing for a more authentic message. Also, remember to get their feedback so you can grow and expand the program based on the brand ambassador's feedback and experience sharing your messages. Also, getting feedback allows the brand to work with the brand ambassador to engage in other ways like writing blogs, additional social media posts or video messages.

Understanding Your Customer

What do we do to truly include people with disabilities as customers, employees, and shareholders? First, understand the community and remember that disabilities are a natural part of life and that just because you have a disability doesn't mean you cannot add value. Recognize that there are many people who acquire disabilities later in life, which is about 80 percent of the disability population. Many have learned to become problem-solvers to work around the non-inclusive world that's been created. Making the efforts to include persons with disabilities as clients, employees, and stakeholders add value to a brand's bottom-line.

Brands often are nervous about working with the community of persons with disabilities. As a strategist and advocate in this community, my best advice is to bring in the experts from the different segments of our community. For example, you don't want to talk about the LGBT community without having people from that community doing the talking because it's hard to be authentic and connect if you are not "from" that community.

You really want all the stakeholders to be engaged. I think there's a lot of fear of stakeholders (ironically enough), but with the successes that we're seeing, it's obvious that it works. I think Tommy Hilfiger is a wonderful example of a brand that listened to a good pitch by the community of people with disabilities with

Runway of Dreams to create adaptive clothing. They said, "Ok, we'll do this, but we don't know how to get to the community." They then looked and found an appropriate and relevant way to do that. That line sold out faster than any other line they've had. Kudos to Tommy Hilfiger and that brand for being the first. There is something to be said for being the first.

I also would ask companies, if you are employing people with disabilities in the United States, in the United Kingdom, in Europe, in Australia, please help me understand why you're not doing it in Egypt and in Singapore. Why aren't you doing it in Kenya, Sharjah, Panama, Thailand or Myanmar? Our community could perceive this to mean your brand only cares about employing people with disabilities if it's a compliance issue and there's a threat of litigation.

There are so many brand nuances that have to be considered. There are amazing resources, but I think that we're in the infancy of understanding how to help brands tell your stories in ways that the community and all the different locations perceive your brand's identity.

I often tell audiences from my community that we have a lot more influence on a brand than we realize. Once, when speaking at the National Down Syndrome Congress[49], I said to this audience, "If only us 4,000 families, started writing letters to CEOs of companies thanking them for including us, think of the power this would have." These efforts could make a massive dif-

---

[49] https://www.ndsccenter.org/

ference with a huge number of letters — now that is real impact! I tell my community that brands do care about what we think. They want us as customers and employees, and we can help their brand by speaking up and letting them know why we support their brand and how they can work with us to make a difference.

Here is an article that shows how a corporate brand and new technologies helped a family in Hong Kong when they lost their son with Down syndrome.

A lost boy and a father's search: how Microsoft technology helped solve a four-year mystery

written by Deborah Bach, 31 May, 2017[50]

On a hot morning in June 2012, Junxiu Wang and his son awoke in the city of Guangzhou, northwest of Hong Kong, and started their day.

Wang was working a short-term job in Guangzhou and had taken his 14-year-old son, Yesong, with him. The pair ate breakfast; then Wang went to use the bathroom. When he came out, Yesong was gone. The father was immediately worried. Yesong, his middle child, had Down syndrome and was unable to speak.

Wang called the boy's aunt, thinking he might have gone to visit her, but he wasn't there. Growing increasingly anxious, he went to a nearby subway station and asked if anyone had seen his son. A vendor and a security guard reported seeing a boy who looked like Yesong carrying a bag. Wang's fears intensified. If his son ventured very far away, he knew, he would not be able to find his way back.

It would be almost four agonizing years until Wang found out what happened to his son. The answer would involve an exhaustive search, a dedicated nonprofit director, a popular Chi-

50 https://news.microsoft.com/features/lost-boy-fathers-search-microsoft-technology-helped-solve-four-year-mystery/

nese reality show, Microsoft facial recognition technology and a father who never gave up hope.

And their story was just the beginning. The technology is now helping other families find much-needed answers and has powerful potential for addressing an issue that has long plagued China. There are 64,000 cases on the website of Baobei Huijia (Baby Come Home), a leading nonprofit organization launched in 2007 that is dedicated to finding missing children.

In 2015, Eric Zhou was thinking about how technology might be used to more effectively combat human trafficking. Zhou is a Shanghai-based senior business intelligence manager for the Digital Crimes Unit in Microsoft's Corporate, External & Legal Affairs group in China, which uses data analytics to fight cybercrime and protect vulnerable populations, including children. He came up with a project for Microsoft's annual worldwide employee Hackathon, enlisting his friend Kevin Liu from the Microsoft Support Engineering Group to develop an application that could help find China's missing children.

The effort resulted in the creation of Photo Missing Children, or PhotoMC, an application designed to help find missing children through Microsoft's face recognition application program interface (API). The Microsoft Face API is a cloud-based service that uses advanced algorithms to scan images of faces for identifying features and determines the likelihood that two faces belong to the same person. It can scan a database of thousands of faces and return a list of possible matches within seconds. The API analyzes 27 different facial characteristics and can identify a person across multiple photos, even at different angles and with varying facial expressions.

In the days after Yesong disappeared, Junxiu Wang searched at subway stations and youth shelters in the area. He walked the streets of Guangzhou, desperately hoping to find his son. But in a city of more than 14 million, the chances of spotting him were almost nonexistent.

The anguished father put notices in newspapers and on television. He contacted China's Ministry of Civil Affairs in Beijing and asked for help. Weeks and months stretched by with no leads, but Wang clung to the belief that his son was still alive. And as long as Yesong was alive, Wang would not stop looking for his boy.

Yesong had been missing about three years when Wang found Baby Come Home's website and decided to go visit Zhang to ask for her help. In July 2015, he took a train from Guangzhou to Tonghua City in northeast China, almost 1,900 miles away. Wang arrived at the organization's office exhausted and soaked, carrying a large jackfruit and a box of taro as gifts. After he left, Zhang opened the jackfruit and discovered it was rotten. She wondered how long the father had traveled to get there.

"It made our hearts ache to see him like that," she says, recalling how employees' eyes would fill with tears at the thought of Wang.

Six months after Wang's visit, in January 2016, China's Ministry of Civil Affairs launched a new website to publish information about children living in shelters across the country. Baby Come Home ran the photo of Yesong that his father provided against 13,000 images on the government site, and within seconds, PhotoMC came up with a list of 20 possible matches. One was a boy living in a government-run shelter in the Panyu district of Guangdong City, about 24 miles from where Yesong went missing. Zhang wondered, could the boy be Yesong?

The father looked at the matching photos and immediately identified his son. He provided a DNA sample, which was matched against a sample from the boy at the shelter. Arrangements were made to bring Wang and the boy together on the popular Chinese television show "Waiting for Me." The show, which runs on China's predominant state broadcaster, China Central Television (CCTV), aims to help people find missing children or other loved ones and is produced in partnership with Baby Come Home. The audience and the relative wait in suspense for the opening of a large set of doors, behind which is either the missing person or a police officer who discusses the unsuccessful search.

In February 2016, Wang sat in a chair on the show's stage, his hands clasped nervously in his lap. The doors opened slowly to reveal Yesong, who by that time was 17. Wang exhaled audibly and crossed the stage, crying as he clasped his son to him. At first, Yesong didn't recognize his father, Wang says. But within a month, he says, Yesong readjusted to being home with his parents and two siblings and is now doing well.

Yesong was the first missing child found with the help of PhotoMC, but the application has since helped find four other missing boys in China, and several other possible matches are being followed up on and verified.

One of the boys, a developmentally disabled 17-year-old, was lost in April 2015 in Beijing and had been living in a shelter. Baby Come Home found him with PhotoMC, and on April 28 he went home with his parents.

Mainstream

It's really interesting that leaders like Sandy Carter, Vice President at Amazon Web Services and formerly the Chief Digital Officer for IBM, are not only focusing on the technology, but also how people have to understand this technology from an ecosystem as well as diverse team's perspective. This creates an enormous linkage between innovation, tech, and diversity — the team "training" the software incorporates its paradigms into the coding, so if that team is biased, then the software is biased.

If a company does not have a diverse team, the output may have the wrong results. Take the instance of Mattel programming the Barbie doll to talk to girls. According to Carter, Mattel actually did an amazing job on conversational AI. They had Barbie be able to answer questions about outer space and the red dust on Mars. However, one of the areas that were insufficient was careers. It would respond to the girl's question about a non-programmed "girl job" (such as a data scientist) with, "What about a career in fashion?"

The team that trained Barbie to have these conversations had limits on what careers are "appropriate" for girls — it put the responses and then the girls in a box. If the team building the infrastructure isn't diverse, then the outcome of the most innovative arenas of corporate development is stifled. This can happen with gender issues, race, abilities, or any topic that we know could have an inherent unconscious bias.

Sandy Carter also highlighted the parallel with Virtual Reality as it is often embedded with Artificial Intelligence. Most people have heard there are side effects of dizziness and nauseous. However, they have been working on lessening the side effects only using male feedback. Just as heart attack symptoms are different for men than women, the way that women and men get nauseous is actually different. The innovation of Virtual Reality AI has been programmed and trained only from the male perspective.

It's unlikely that the teams training this AI infrastructure were trying to leave people out of the equation; it was just accidental. But when issues like these are identified, these are the times that we can actually change society. As we are going through these major innovation changes in society, mainstream is changing. We have to ensure that the innovations emerging are reflecting these improvements and we are holding companies accountable for diversity at all levels of your business.

I've been in diversity workshops where the facilitator will list the components of their idea of diversity, and all participants list their ideas, and nobody mentions disabilities. I once sat listening to see how long it was going to take for somebody in this packed room to include disability, and it didn't happen. When they were about to close down the discussion, I raised my hand and said it, and people suddenly did the head nod, "Oh yeah, yeah, yeah." Until it's a mainstream consideration, we still have our work cut out for us.

What I also think is interesting is the difficulty for corporations to really understand the benefits of diversity and embrace it in your corporate culture. I often find that when you're talking about these diverse groups that you're only speaking to the already-diverse parts of the business. These niche areas don't seem to have a lot of resources (personnel, executive, and monetary support), or a lot of support from upper management. The employees doing the right thing with diversity get disenfranchised, which hurts the entire company. A failure for everyone is certainly not the way to build a cohesive, progressive corporate culture.

It is critical to figure out how we have the conversations without scaring off groups. There is no value in leaving any category out of this conversation. At the same time, considering the uneven representation of a certain category in any workplace is important, such as the staggering number of men working in technologies as opposed to women. We need leaders to have these conversations on innovation, but remember what it means to keep the outcome mainstream. For mainstream output to occur, the input must come from more than one small slice of the pie.

As a matter of fact, many people with disabilities, especially technologists with disabilities, bring a real unique mindset to these types of conversations because they've had to travel a different path than people without disabilities. Inherently, the world is usually not very accessible to an individual who is profoundly deaf, uses a wheelchair, is blind, or acquires a mental health disability or a traumatic brain injury. These individuals are having to navigate the world using different parts of their brain and therefore are problem solvers.

6

Best Practices

"Brands benefit when they demonstrate social inclusion. They benefit from public perception, and they benefit from the goodwill of the communities they are including. There is ever-greater awareness about the large community of people with disabilities as an under-tapped market."

-Sara Basson, Accessibility Evangelist

Introduction

In this final chapter, we will take the previous data and tie it together and examine best practices. The good news is that communities are learning to connect in different ways as technology and communications have improved. The community of persons with disabilities is no exception. We are finding our path and our voices and breaking down silos.

So how does a brand effectively include persons with disabilities into a customer and employee base? – Is it possible for a brand to be successful with this community? Is there value in including people with disabilities that might not have been previously considered?

Though attempts have been made, the problem is the laws, standards, and societal expectations are often considered confusing, unobtainable, and fluid. In addition, and rightly so, people with disabilities are demanding they have the same civil rights as other members of society and members of this community are voicing their frustration on avenues like social media.

Attacks of brands via social media for not including this population in your workforce, not accommodating us, not retaining us in the workforce, and for not including us as customers are increasingly frequent in occurrence. Sometimes the attacks have merit; sometimes there is more to the story. The bottom line is that no brand or person for that matter likes being attacked on social media. Many of the brands with which I work want to include the community of persons with disabilities, but do not know how to tell their disability inclusion and accessibility stories. They fear that they have not done enough and are often embarrassed by their lack of progress. Currently, if a brand does not take the lead with telling its own disability inclusion and accessibility stories, the community will fill in the blanks themselves — rarely is that good for the company.

The good news is that brands can successfully embrace this enormous market. These strategies can also be used to include other diverse communities and to support Corporate Social Responsibility (CSR) and other Social Impact programs.

Brand Loyalty

Corporate Brands must be part of the conversations, and that means engaging effectively with communities. Brands must humanize your brands, and that means helping consumers remember that your products are made by and for human beings, and yes some of those people should and will include persons with disabilities.

Ten Steps for Successful Brand and Marketing Campaigns

The most valuable asset to your firm must be your brand. Your brand includes employees, customers, shareholders, investors, and supply chain. Here are ten steps to assure you have a successful and engaging brand and marketing campaign.

1. **Define Clear Goals Campaign.** Understand the Why, What and How. Why are we doing this? How will things be different at the initiative's end? Will we have new guidelines to make it easier to communicate consistently about our brand to our customers and employees? Will we clearly articulate who we are and what we stand for? Will our website work on mobile devices? Remember to have an endpoint for the campaign.

2. **Create clear responsibilities.** Acknowledge that your investment will require staff time, not just writing checks.

It›s a collaborative process. Identify an internal person to be the direct contact for the branding firm--a «make it happen» person with superior organization skills.

3. **Use a disciplined process with realistic benchmarks.** Agree on what the brand stands for before any creative work is done. Use marketing tools to ensure that key decision makers agree on your brand's essence, its competitive advantage, your target market, and your value proposition.

4. **Stay customer-centric.** The best brand decisions can only be made with the customer's needs and experiences in mind. See the world through the eyes of your customers.

5. **Commit to a small decision group at the beginning of the process.** Never bring in decision-makers in the middle of the process. Key decision-makers must be present throughout the process and at all key decision points.

6. **Determine your readiness to make a commitment.** Is your company ready to invest the time, capital, and human resources to revitalize your brand? Readiness is a critical success factor.

7. **The executive team must endorse the marketing campaign and brand.** There must be a strong mandate from the top. If the commitment to revitalize the brand is tepid, it will fizzle in the middle. Do you have a plan and a disciplined process that is easy to understand?

8. **Determine how you will measure success.** Consider benefits like employee engagement, and a more efficient, cost-effective

marketing toolbox. Communicate that it›s everyone's job to protect and grow the brand asset.

9. **Launch internally first, then externally to key stakeholders.** Remember to communicate why you made these changes and what they mean. Thoughtfully consider your list of stakeholders as you plan your launch. Make sure that all of your vendors have access to the new guidelines.

10. **Demonstrate—don't declare—why customers should choose you over others.** Seize every opportunity to communicate your value, and to radically differentiate your brand from others. Identify touchpoints where you can build trust, attract new customers, create buzz, and inspire customer loyalty.

Interview with August de los Reyes

I had the pleasure to interview August de los Reyes[54], Head of Design and Research at Pinterest, on my show, Human Potential at Work. In the interview, August discusses accessibility through better design and why he left his position at Microsoft, as Head of Design for Xbox, to work at Pinterest. August also discusses disability as a design problem and why better design benefits everyone. He has been a designer for nearly 30 years and now plays a key role on the Pinterest team of about 75 people who help people discover, share and engage with other people who have similar interests.

During his tenure at Microsoft August fell and broke his back and sustained a spinal cord injury. He now uses a wheelchair to get around and tells how his new life allowed him to tap into his design obsession, especially in the sense of "understanding a pain point or a challenging situation or a base dissatisfaction with the status quo." He was able to tap into design in a way that he had never considered. When he looked at his situation with a design lens, he wondered how he could improve his own life experience and that of others at the same time. He felt fortunate to be working in technology and knew his work scaled to hundreds and millions of people around the globe. He decided to marry his interest in design with his current situation and started exploring inclusion and diversity in the consumer technology space.

[54] http://www.ruhglobal.com/80-pinterests-head-design-research-accessibility-transformation/

August found that it was all about the optics and researched work done by Hungarian psychologist named Mihaly Csikszentmihalyi[55]. Dr. Csikszentmihalyi, the Distinguished Professor of Psychology and Management at Claremont Graduate University, recognized and named the psychological concept of flow, a highly focused mental state. August found his work profound and was very interested in his talks on flow. He found that when he was in a flow state and engaged in a meaningful activity, suddenly his sense of time got distorted as he focused on the activity. August was able to tap into this flow with his work at Microsoft and Pinterest.

He found it especially helpful at Pinterest. Many people consider Pinterest a social media platform. However, August disagrees and feels Pinterest is different from a lot of the social media services that they are often compared with. Why? Adding pins, or pinning is a solitary activity. The user or 'pinner' is collecting pins for many reasons including travel ideas, product ideas for their home or family, or services/products that inspire action today and in the future. But what they all have in common is that they are collected for the user, not for an observer of the user such as one's friends on a social network.

> *"I think that's a very different thing than a social network. The objectives of the two are different. On a social network, you upload photos for other people to like. Pinterest, on the other hand, is self-serving."*
>
> -Ben Silbermann Co-Founder of Pinterest

[55] https://en.wikipedia.org/wiki/Mihaly_Csikszentmihalyi

August said, "What is this magic behind Pinterest? My research team and I looked at the early days of Pinterest. As with anything, it's usually a good place to start at the beginning. In 2010, when Pinterest took off, suddenly, just out of the blue, millions and millions of people started using Pinterest. They followed very similar demographic patterns showing there was a latent unmet need that Pinterest filled.

"I happen to know people who fell into that demographic, so I asked both of them this question: What was your life like before Pinterest and what was your life like after Pinterest? The first person told me that she never considered herself a creative person. After Pinterest, she realized she's absolutely creative. The second person I talked to, and I'm going to paraphrase, was living her life in a kind of quiet desperation, because she was going through the motions, getting the kids ready for school, fixing, cleaning up the house, doing a little decorating, and then trying to decide what to cook for dinner. She said she was just going through this day by day and she felt like she wasn't really good at any of it. She said after she started using Pinterest, she learned to assert herself into her own day to day experience."

August was intrigued about how platforms like Pinterest or even gaming platforms like Xbox supported the inner dialogue. The journey can be about self-discovery and discovering your own tastes and preferences. August believes this is where the magic happens.

August noted: "Every pin is a possibility to change your life offline. Your experience doesn't end in the app; rather it's a starting point. Even if it's something as simple as adding a couple of drops of Tabasco sauce to a hollandaise sauce to give it a kick, that's just a microform of self-expression. When I was at Xbox, I would argue, in the world of design and technology, being the head of design for Xbox is one of the sexiest positions in our industry. People asked me, 'Why on earth would you leave that behind to go work at Pinterest?' I mean, there's some superficial things like when I tell people that I work at Xbox, people would say, 'Oh, my husband, son, brother, nephew would want to meet you.' But now when I say, 'I work at Pinterest,' they say, 'My wife, daughter, niece wants to meet you.'

"Here's the subtle difference. I think one of the humanistic aspects of video games is that the whole point of a video game, the whole goal of a video game is just to feel something. The emotions that people feel when they play the game, whether it's accomplishment or defeat, victory, frustration, achievement, all of those emotions are absolutely authentic. They're very real. Except they occur in a mental space that is just the game. The thing about Pinterest is, Pinterest is a kind of game also, where one can feel these emotions of curiosity, exploration, warmth, support, hope, optimism. Except the difference is, once you turn off your computer or turn off your phone, you're still feeling those emotions, and they're actually impacting your life away from your computer or your device."

August also noted that one of the design principles that he embraces is to think universally but to act personally. When he looks at challenges, particularly around the accessibility and inclusion, people can often quickly become overwhelmed.

"This feeling can lead to option paralysis or just getting so caught up you don't do anything. To address that, even taking action against your own personal situation, you can assume that what's good for your situation is probably helpful to millions and millions of other people's situations as well."

After his accident, August went back to work and had a new boss. August explains the situation:

"I had returned from being away in the hospital and going through physical rehabilitation for about six months. When I returned to Microsoft, there was this massive corporate restructuring, and I returned to a new boss. What I found is all the heads of design for each of the product units now reported to him, I being one of them. He asked us to come up with what are the common threads or the principles or our point of view that we want to assert across the entire spectrum of products, from the cool, cutting-edge stuff like Xbox and HoloLens to Windows.

"There's a whole span of products. We were tasked with coming up with what we have in common. One of the areas that really resonated with me is an ocean of universal design. In other words, one of the things that all these products have in common is that we serve hundreds of millions of people. Including Pinterest, as well, by the way. Coming back to Microsoft. Looking at universal design, for whatever reason, designers find it challenging to think about accessibility, maybe because it's not sexy or what have you. But given that we design for such huge populations, it's incumbent on us to design for everyone.

"In researching universal design, we actually stumbled upon the re-definition of disability by the World Health Organization in 1982. It shifted the definition of disability from the medical to the societal model. In other words, disability is not a result of some sort of physiological phenomenon. Rather, it is a mismatch between an individual's level of ability and the environment and objects, which she or he interacts with.

"The damning thing about this observation is that disability is actually designed, whether it's an oversight or a lack of consideration, but the fact that some experience is not accessible was designed into the building of the product or the experience. In critiquing accessibility, suddenly this approach of inclusive design actually made design sexy and creative and really appealing. Because if you look at the history of inclusive design...

"Well, let me back up a bit. The guiding principle around inclusive design is if you design for a specific person for their ability difference, you can assume that it benefits everyone else. Because there's no such thing as normal. Everyone. Every one of us experiences an ability difference at some point in our life, whether you're missing an arm or you broke your arm and it's in a cast, or you're just carrying groceries and a baby. You've lost the use of your arm. If we design for that extreme case, then we can assume it benefits everyone else.

"In looking at the history of inclusive design, there are a lot of examples where the intent was to help someone with an ability difference, and the outcome is it benefits everyone. A great example of this is the remote control. Back in the 50's, the original intent of the remote control was so people who had some sort of mobility difference who couldn't get up and cross the living room to change the channel, back when you had to do that. Now let's jump ahead a few decades later, the remote control is a de facto feature of every TV, everywhere. And it gets better.

"That was a kind of "aha!" moment, and as you start looking deeper into it, you find an entire history. Like, Alexander Graham Bell[56] discovered the telephone because he was trying to help the deaf. The person who invented the keyboard was an Italian aristocrat who was in love with this Contessa who was blind, and since she couldn't write letters legibly on her own, he invented the keyboard so that she could write her letters.

"Even email protocol's Vint Cerf[57] at Google, who's hard of hearing and whose wife is deaf, he helped develop early email protocols so that they could bypass relay services. Someone out of IBM with a cognitive difference invented the database. Even everyday objects like the bendable straw[58]. Joseph Friedman, a father, noticed his daughter couldn't drink her milkshake when it was sitting high up on the counter, and the straw was just too hard for her to reach. When he went home, he put a screw in the straw and wrapped wire around it and now she could do that. We see things like the electric toothbrush and Oxo GoodGrips[59], which Sam Farber created when he noticed his wife Betsey was having trouble comfortably holding her peeler due to arthritis.

---

[56] http://www.history.com/topics/inventions/alexander-graham-bell
[57] https://en.wikipedia.org/wiki/Vint_Cerf
[58] https://en.wikipedia.org/wiki/Joseph_Friedman
[59] https://www.oxo.com/our-brands

"One thing about all these innovations is even though their original intent was for someone with an ability difference, we don't even question that it benefits everyone. It circumvents the whole notion of accessibility. Rather, this is just straight up innovation. It's straight up invention. But here's the beautiful thing about all of those stories. Every single one of those stories is a love story. We get blindsided by it because of other systems in which we exist. You brought up the notion of authenticity, and I think the reason why these innovations and inventions are so pure, and they're so effective is because they were born out of very authentic, humanistic concerns for someone else."

August proves my point that disabilities are a normal part of life. We can all add value to society and the workforce.

Advocate

The community of persons with disabilities and employers that are including us need to work together to help society understand that persons with disabilities can add value to society. I applaud all the efforts Microsoft is making to assure they are employing qualified persons with disabilities in all areas of the company.[60] To join this movement, your brand needs to reach out to the people with the knowledge of what abilities can be brought to the table and keep the conversation in the language of business rather than the language of fear or policy, in order to become the best advocate for inclusion.

There needs to be a way that we get beyond management considering what is the cost of accommodations, what policy says we need to accommodate, how much slower is my line going to run when I accommodate. It needs to be about more than this. Every person is worth it. More people need to speak out about the great reasons to diversify and to be inclusive and be authentic.

A conscious effort needs to change corporate culture to identify talent in a better manner for all people, not only for those with visible or invisible disabilities. Making the jobs about expectations and better service or better products for customers is why companies are in business. But if you don't realize it or aren't

---

60 https://www.microsoft.com/en-us/diversity/inside-microsoft/cross-disability/hiring.aspx

asking what the company could be doing better, how can you expect to keep up with and contribute to this evolution?

Jenny shared transparently that 17 of 23 applicants with disabilities had previously applied to Microsoft and not been hired because of the way they were interviewing applicants. Now they have a Microsoft "academy" hands-on test where the applicant is evaluated on their skills to accomplish tasks and where they can best be placed. The reason for all of this is technology. When you're doing something to help a segment of the population (since persons with disabilities are lumped as a minority segment with a billion people), it benefits everyone.

Many times, people are told they are their own best advocates when it comes to raises or promotions, or even just selling themselves for a job in an interview. But if the corporate culture is missing the keys to ask the right questions for the success of the individual (and thus the business), no one wins. I remember one time I was interviewed by a very large credit card company and they really wanted me because I had this great background. I just really brought a lot to the table. During the interview process, they had me do an algebra test. Wow, really? I didn't understand at the time why being the director required me to know algebra. They didn't hire me, and to this day I'm not sure what algebra had to do with the position. I believe they lost out because they tested a detail and didn't embrace the whole person. We want diversity in the workforce. You want people that use their brains differently.

EMPATHY IS POWER

How fathering a son with disabilities helped Microsoft's CEO transform the company[61]

BY JASON WARD

I'm convinced that a leader's character and how he leads are intricately intertwined. Who a person is in his professional capacity is simply who he is. And that person's character shapes a company's culture for better or worse.

We all know or have seen someone with a disability. But how many of us have stopped to look at life through that person's eyes? How many of us have contemplated the profound challenge even a small staircase poses to someone who uses a wheelchair? Or who among us has considered that the window to the internet, the displays on our devices, is a barrier to the visually impaired?

As we complain about and compare the accuracy of digital keyboards, people with quadriplegia wish for the ability to merely use a keyboard. Most of us don't give much thought to these things. And when we do, it is often a brief contemplation because we feel uncomfortable and sometimes helpless to do anything about it. But what about large companies like Microsoft?

---

61 https://www.windowscentral.com/how-fathering-son-disability-helped-ceo-satya-nadella-transform-microsoft-through-empathy

How does a leader shape a culture that is empathetic and sees the needs of its employees, teams and all of its customers?

Learning to see through others' eyes

A leader's character sets the tone and the atmosphere of a company's culture. That culture affects how team members feel about themselves in their work environments and how they feel about and interact with others.

A company without a clear vision of others, who they are and what they need will have a clinical, anesthetic approach in its service to its employees and customers. There will be a disconnect. A company without the ability to perceive a need through a customer's eyes will struggle for relevance and will have more failures than successes. Its ability to have a meaningful impact on the lives of people of varying levels of ability will also be limited. A company that has profound human resources, a pool of sharp minds, broad technological reach and billions of dollars in capital has the power to help the disabled and the disadvantaged in a way charitable efforts of lesser means cannot.

Microsoft has had many profound world-changing successes as well as many notable and image-damaging failures. Over 40 years ago, founders Bill Gates and Paul Allen set out to put a PC on every desk and in every home. These visionaries saw a need that PCs would help businesses and individuals fulfill. The PC on every desk and in every home goal has been more or less achieved in most developed regions. But Microsoft's internal structure has been notoriously plagued by a toxic environment of infighting and competition that for a time hurt its ability to effectively serve its customers needs.

Self-destructive culture

The competitiveness and fear of failure that permeated Microsoft's culture were exacerbated by the leadership styles of Gates and Steve Ballmer, the company's first two CEOs.

Current CEO Satya Nadella[62] remarked in a recent interview that both these men exercised a leadership approach where they initiated a conversation by first acknowledging the "20 things you did wrong."

This type of leadership during and in the wake of a very public antitrust battle drew the company's focus inward, as it began to walk on eggshells to address its own needs to avoid further infractions, Microsoft lost sight of customers and their needs.

The company was failing at the expression of empathy, the ability to see things through another's eyes, until Nadella whose eyes were opened by his son Zain, who has Cerebral Palsy, took the helm.

Zain and Microsoft's cultural change

Nadella's oldest son, Zain was born in 1996 with severe Cerebral Palsy. Nadella said this of the life-altering event:

---

[62] https://en.wikipedia.org/wiki/Satya_Nadella

"If anything, I should be doing everything to put myself in [Zain's] shoes, given the privilege I have to be able to help him ... empathy is a massive part of who I am today ... I distinctly remember who I was as a person before and after."

This shift in Nadella's outlook led him to become the executive sponsor for Microsoft's community group for staff members with disabilities years before becoming CEO. He continues to meet with the group and speaks at its annual event. Nadella's seeing the world through the eyes of his son with limited mobility has helped him see the need for Microsoft's products to be accessible to all and made him a more empathetic leader.

Nadella's mission for Microsoft is to empower every person and company to achieve more. A passion to give people of varying abilities the tools, to empower them, to achieve their goals is a mission birthed from empathy. Nadella has worked to change Microsoft's competitive culture to one that embraces these values internally so that they are reflected with its customers.

Failure is now embraced as a learning experience; taking chances is an opportunity to learn. I can imagine that his encouraging his son to take chances and supporting him through failures and successes greatly contributes to this empathetic leadership style.

Change happens

Many Microsoft watchers may focus on Microsoft's high-profile failures and miss the broader effects the shift in leadership has brought the company. When Nadella took the helm, the company was viewed as headed toward irrelevance. It has since more than recovered, and its shares now exceed previous peaks.

Nadella's approach to leadership is more inclusive than that of his predecessors. He encourages relationships with former competitors like Linux, DropBox and other tech companies with whom it now collaborates. Perhaps raising Zain opened Nadella's eyes to the network of support Microsoft will need to remain relevant long after he leaves the post as CEO.

Microsoft's ability to beneficially affect the lives of individuals with disabilities given its position is not lost on the company. During a senior leadership team meeting in June, Microsoft engineers were video conferenced in so that a prototype of an app for visually impaired people could be tested. That's just one example of how Microsoft is working to use its resources to assist those with disabilities.

Making an impact

During its Build 2016 developer conference, a blind Microsoft employee demonstrated AI-driven smartglasses that use Microsoft's Cognitive Services to help the blind navigate the world. The software can recognize facial expressions, activity and more. This app, now called Seeing AI, was made available on iOS this year.

During Microsoft's Hackathon event a team of individuals embraced the seemingly mundane task to make Windows easier to navigate for the visually impaired. Though not as exciting a task as some other hackathon endeavors, imagine the impact this will have for millions of people around the world who may otherwise not have been able to use Windows.

Microsoft OneNote has also been used to help children with dyslexia read and spell. HoloLens has helped surgeons with spinal surgeries.

Eye tracking technology has been used to help people with ALS navigate their world. This same tech is part of Windows and empowers people to navigate Windows with just their eyes. Imagine a mind trapped in a body unable to verbally express one's thoughts or move. Imagine being released from that prison by technology that allows one's eye, the windows to the soul, to express oneself using Windows.

No leader or company is perfect. But Microsoft has shifted toward a more empathetic company in the three years since Nadella has taken the helm. How might that empathy continue to translate into how it interacts with consumers and meets customer needs in the years to come?

Special thanks to Jason Ward for giving us permission to print this article in this book.

Rethink

We need to train people and educate everyone including persons with disabilities to add value to today's workforce. This is the Future of Work – Inclusion. These technologies are improving the lives of people with severe disabilities not only in the workforce but also in everyday living.

Technologies can help persons with disabilities and the Aging in Place Market to become more involved, stay involved longer, and be more meaningfully engaged in the workforce and in our communities. Technology (just like any source of power) needs to be used for the right reason, to address Human Potential and spread empathy in the form of problem-solving so no one is left out of the community. Imagine being in a Spanish-speaking country and not knowing the language. With technology now, we can have real-time live translation and solve this type of problem. And that's just the tip of the iceberg. We can now create prostheses through 3-D printing for poor people anywhere - in Africa, India, China, in South and Central America. I'm a very hopeful person, so I'm very excited about the opportunity to improve and embrace humanity by allowing technology to complement our brains as well as humanity as a whole.

I had the pleasure to interview[63] John Kemp, President and CEO of The Viscardi Center; we discussed how he has was able to flourish despite being born with a disability and losing

---

[63] http://www.ruhglobal.com/69-educating-employing-empowering-persons-disabilities/

his mother at a young age. John shares how his father was able to help him become more resilient and discusses what needs to change when it comes to improving employment outcomes for persons with disabilities. John also discusses the success rate that the Viscardi Center has when it comes to educating, employing, and empowering persons with disabilities.

I asked John what it was like to be born with a disability. "Only 17% of us start out our lives with our disabilities, and so people join the disability ranks by accidents, illness, injuries... They just never anticipated this, and so they join, and yes, that can cause them some high anxiety and fearfulness, but at the same time, any good business person would say, 'Why would I lop off 20% of an applicant pool? If I could add 20% more people into the applicant pool and skim the very best people off the top and include some of those folks with disabilities, wouldn't I be a better business for it?'"

The answer is, absolutely, you would. And the fact that we have money, not a lot of money, but some money, would make you want us as a customer, I would think. Because you really don't ever have enough customers, right? We want to be the customer of choice. We want to be the customer that's wanted and treated with respect, the consumer that a business would want.

John adds, "We look at that, and then we think about corporate social responsibility and really want to be part of the CSR programs that companies have where they can include disability on businesses as part of their supply chain and in addition to the employment and looking at people as customers or consumers that can be part of the supply chain and nourish the communities in which they live and work. There are a lot of good reasons that corporations should really be thinking about the brand that they have and the brand identity that they have, and remember, people with disabilities really want to be their customer and their employee." John Kemp[64]

We are making progress, but many corporate brands are not meaningfully including the community of persons with disabilities. I have been honored to consult with the United Nations International Labour Organization (ILO) and Global Compact. They created a guide for corporate brands to understand the rights of persons with disabilities and how corporations can benefit by including this demographic. I was honored to be a contributor to this amazing resource. "Guide for business on the rights of persons with disabilities - How business can respect and support the rights of persons with disabilities and benefit from inclusion", developed jointly by the UN Global Compact (UNGC) and the ILO.[65]

"When we think of people with disabilities, we often think of sympathy. What I say, "It's not sympathy. It is empathy." You have to put yourself in his place, "What kind of service I should receive? Why always they would like to help me? They don't want to make me help myself." This is huge difference between looking at a guy with a

[64] https://www.viscardicenter.org

[65] https://www.unglobalcompact.org/library/5381

disability and trying to help him to go through whatever agony he is going through, or you are looking at him and seeing where is his strength points and try to help him to be totally independent using these strength points. This is always what I say, that co-creation and empathy is the key success to your, whatever, framework or strategy."

-Engineer Suhail M Al-Almaee, Executive Director of Projects Sector, Tatweer Education Holding Company, Kingdom of Saudi Arabia

Best Messaging and Advertisements

It is rare for a brand to have the opportunity to reach out to an underserved, loyal audience that has the depth, reach, and economic power of this community. I believe that future innovations are going to keep coming from corporate brands as opposed to governments. Brands have the potential now to reach anybody in the world. Corporations need to think about your brand identity, your inclusiveness, your openness, your transparency, and how you empower the best people you can possibly find as employees. It's about assuring all customers have full access to services and products as brand stories are shared, so we understand brands are not only focused on profit but also adding value to communities and the world.

Here are some examples from companies that know how to communicate the real story:

- Hillary Clinton uses silent auto-play to include the community of people who are deaf.[66]
- Honey Maid depicts an aunt with a disability caring for her niece.[67]
- Maltesers, a candy brand, features people with disabilities telling amusing and awkward everyday life stories.[68]
- Lego's toy line up now includes a man in a wheelchair mini-figure.[69]
- Intel's film series, "Look Inside," uses an ad spot featuring a mountain climber who is blind.[70]
- Guinness depicts a wheelchair basketball game.[71]
- SunTrust features an actor with autism playing a character with autism and his family doing some financial planning together.[72]

---

[66] http://www.adweek.com/brand-marketing/hillary-clinton-just-made-great-use-silent-autoplay-facebook-twitter-and-instagram-173610/
[67] http://www.adweek.com/creativity/honey-maids-latest-wholesome-family-features-disabled-aunt-and-her-niece-166102/
[68] http://www.adweek.com/creativity/british-candy-brand-will-air-funny-ad-entirely-sign-language-no-subtitles-173288/
[69] http://www.adweek.com/creativity/lego-unveils-its-first-disabled-minifigure-good-week-inclusivity-169305/
[70] http://www.adweek.com/brand-marketing/ad-day-worlds-most-amazing-mountain-climber-stars-intels-latest-spot-155534/
[71] http://www.adweek.com/creativity/wheelchair-basketball-ad-guinness-wins-buzzer-beater-152216/
[72] http://www.adweek.com/creativity/actor-autism-stars-suntrust-ad-about-parents-planning-retirement-three-148168/

- Dolores Cortés, swimwear designer, features a 10-month-old girl model with Down syndrome.[73]
- Target features a 10-year-old girl model with cerebral palsy.[74]
- Wonderbra features a Belgian designer whose lower left arm ends at the elbow modeling a bra.[75]

Brands are breaking through the inclusivity ceiling and creating social impact that speaks to consumers, increases profitability and changes the world. Your next step is to get a vision of your brand as a leader in this evolution of world culture and take action to bring that vision to fruition.

The following footnote links are commercials made to show what the world would be like if it was created only for people with disabilities.

1: Video: A world made for disabilities by EDF[76]. This is an English translation of a French-language commercial for EDF showing people without disabilities trying to live in a world made for those with disabilities.

---

[73] http://www.adweek.com/creativity/miami-girl-down-syndrome-face-swimwear-ad-campaign-142122/
[74] http://www.dailymail.co.uk/femail/article-4787978/Model-Emily-Prior-cerebral-palsy-opens-career.html
[75] http://www.adweek.com/creativity/wonderbra-ad-updated-disabilities-psa-12052/
[76] https://www.youtube.com/watch?v=RsuKxY_9f_8

2: Clip from "Talk" by the Disability Rights Commission (UK)[77]. This clip from the UK follows a man without disabilities who has a job interview in a world designed to serve only the disabled.

Bottom-line, it is time for brands to understand the true value of including all communities in your marketing efforts. The world has become more complicated, the news cycles more intense with more reports of 'Fake News' and sometimes unfounded attacks. Brands are getting publicly attacked at alarming rates with little to no way to defend or protect your brand. During these tough and turbulent times, it is more important than ever for you to help create a sense of community support.

It is time for you to reframe marketing challenges and to find new opportunities to really engage with communities. If a brand is aligned and communicating with a community, that community will support and defend you in ways you cannot do for yourselves. This is why, as you pursue new opportunities and growth, it is time to let go of marketing that does not add value to the communities you are trying to serve. It is time to rethink your brand marketing by looking through the lens of community.

You must focus on meeting the needs of the customers. Customers want to feel valued and understood. When a brand focuses on building communities--getting closer to an existing one or helping build new ones--that deliver tangible and emotional value through employees and customers working together

[77] https://www.youtube.com/watch?v=k3AeIFup1qY

to overcome collective challenges, you create a powerful impact that forges emotional bonds. When an existing community like the community of persons with disabilities is valued and strengthened, people who once felt marginalized now find validation. In this way, you build lasting bonds of loyalty, discover new sources of growth and tap into the collective power of community.

As the global community of persons with disabilities finds our voices, the brands that have supported us, told us your stories, assured access for all, and included us by employing and retaining persons with disabilities will reap the rewards.

Do not be Reactive. Be Proactive.

About Debra Ruh

Debra Ruh is a Global Disability Inclusion Strategist, an internationally recognized keynote speaker, and a published author.

Debra has been in this field for 30+ years and is recognized as a solid Thought Leader. Media outlets often contact Debra and ask her to write or participate in articles or white papers. National and Global Organizations that support people with disabilities trust, confide, and ask for her strategic support to grow their organizations.

Her expertise includes the United Nations Convention on the Rights of Persons with Disabilities (CRPD), US Rehabilitation Act of 1973 – Sections 508, 503, and 504, and the American's with Disabilities Act (ADA). She is a seasoned entrepreneur founding three firms including Ruh Global Communications, TecAccess, and Strategic Performance Solutions.

As a world-renowned author, Debra leverages her extensive marketing and technology experience while merging her passion and expertise for inclusion advocacy into books, articles and her regular contributions to the Huffington Post.

Debra's other books include:

Tapping Into HIDDEN Human Capital:
How Leading Global Companies Improve Their Bottom Line by Employing Persons With Disabilities

Find Your Voice Using Social Media

To learn more about Debra, her team and company visit:

RuhGlobal.com

Connect with Debra on Facebook, Twitter, Instagram, LinkedIn, YouTube and Google+ using @debraruh on all social platforms.

Listen to and participate with her online shows at

· Human Potential at Work
humanpotential.libsyn.com/podcast

· AXSChat on Twitter
https://twitter.com/AXSChat

· Global Impact Today worldwide broadcast network.
http://www.ruhglobal.com/global-impact-today/

Made in the USA
Middletown, DE
17 September 2018